"With an authentic voice that res  eri Easter writes like she sings. *Hear* ve emotion guaranteed to touch you in _____ way.
Andy Andrews, New York Times *bestselling author of* The Noticer & The Traveler's Gift

"We listen when she speaks because we know she has something to say. *Hear My Heart* is a savory glimpse of the people and events that have made Sheri Easter one of gospel music's most eloquent and beloved artists."
Janet Paschal, award-winning singer, songwriter, and author

"She's a voice you fall in love with. She has the best outlook on life and is passionate about her call to help others. She's just beautiful inside and out. Everyone is better just being around Sheri Easter. Now we have her heart on pages."
Jason Crabb, Grammy Award-winning artist

"Fighting back tears while writing this, I can honestly say that Sheri Easter is the perfect example of 'GRACE'. I watched her battle breast cancer with boldness and determination. She prayed. She cried. She laughed. She persevered. Sheri will forever be my dear friend and my hero."
Karen Peck Gooch, multiple Grammy Award-nominated artist and President of the Southern Gospel Music Association

"*Hear My Heart* is absolutely beautiful. Through Sheri Easter's triumphs and tragedies, it is the Spirit of her words which empowers her readers to "Stand in the Light" and never miss an opportunity to make a difference in someone else's life. When this story of love is poured into your life… it'll strengthen you, speak to you… and remind you that each day is truly a gift from God."

Rita Cosby, Emmy-winning TV host and New York Times *bestselling author of* Quiet Hero

"I cannot stop reading *Hear My Heart*… Sheri is not only my favorite singer, but she has now become my favorite author with this tender 'American Girl' story of life, love, challenge, and faith."

Joe Bonsall, 38-year member of The Oak Ridge Boys and author of nine books

"Sheri captures 'the heart' as she shares her life's experiences from her heart. Her life as a wife, mother, and singer will inspire you to 'keep singing' when you face the stark realities of everyday living. Her message, her song, and her smile are clearly a result of her faith, her passion, and her determination."

Anne Beiler, founder of Auntie Anne's pretzels, author, and speaker

"I love Jeff & Sheri Easter! I've known them for almost 20 years and what you see is what you get. Sheri has come through one of the toughest times of her life and has chosen to write about it, the good and the bad, in hopes of encouraging someone else. On these pages, she shares the heart that I've come to know. I've asked her many times if she realized how much Jeff loves her...she knows, because he's proven it by being her caregiver when she needed him most."

Mark Lowry, Award-winning comedian, songwriter and member of the Gaither Vocal Band

"Sheri Easter and I go way back—our high school teams competed against each other in youthful days...we both walked the hallowed halls of the University of Georgia...and somewhere along the way we both decided gospel music was where we wanted to be. Little did we know back then that 30 years later each of us would write a book within the span of a short few months. Considering our history, it's only fitting that I wanted Sheri to offer her thoughts about my book; Sheri wanted my thoughts about her book. Never before has a book title been so appropriate. Regardless of what Sheri does in her life, she gives her heart to its purpose, to its very being. She wants to share...she wants to inspire...she wants to encourage. Sheri's heart soars with your triumphs, breaks with your sorrows, and mends with godly understanding—all because she has been there. Find a quiet corner, turn to the next page...and let the heart of my friend speak to you."

Danny Jones, editor-in-chief, Singing News

"In this sweet, engaging memoir, Sheri peels back the layers and generously shares her heart. It is indeed a beautiful sight to behold."
Ronda Rich, bestselling author of What Southern Women Know About Faith

"You've known a corner of Sheri's heart through her music; now you're about to get a piece of it straight from the center. Her words, her stories, her feelings, her faith – it's all here. She has poured out every hard, sincere, and tender moment on these pages. Sheri Easter – the Sweetheart of Gospel Music – a winner in every way."
Don Reid, The Statler Brothers

"Sheri's pages sing with a voice that is authentic and strong, brimming over with love for her family, her life, and her God. Her courageous story embodies the words of Isaiah, 'In quietness and in confidence shall be your strength.'"
Russ and Tori Taff, Grammy Award-winning artist and freelance writer, respectively

"Sheri Easter writes with a down-home style that brings the reader into her world. Her life experiences, the triumphs and trials, are captured in a way that inspires and challenges the heart, and her heart can be heard in each chapter as you read her inspiring story."
Joni Lamb, Daystar Television Network

"When words get in the way, God hears our heart. However, we humans need words. I am so glad my good friend Sheri Easter has put her heart into words. They will be an encouragement to all who read."

Ernie Haase, award-winning artist, Ernie Haase & Signature Sound

"Sheri Easter and I have been friends for over 20 years. She is a woman of great spirit, faith, and courage, whose life has been an inspiration to millions of fans. She is well loved in the music industry, not only for her singing abilities, but also her transparency and in her gift of writing. I know this book will be an encouragement and a blessing to all who read it."

Lily Isaacs, award-winning artists, The Isaacs

"In addition to having one of the most distinctive and signature voices in all of Gospel Music, Sheri Easter is a treasure to Gospel Music because of her always friendly demeanor and her unwavering testimony for Christ. She is a joy to know, and this book will no doubt be an inspiration to all who read it as she tells her life story and gives a personal testimony of how, as written in the words of one of her most popular songs, 'when you slip and reach rope's end, you'll find the hem of his garment.'"

Clarke Beasley, President of the National Quartet Convention

"As I read the entries of Sheri's day-to-day struggles, I think of how precious life is. Tears filled my eyes as I read her words. No matter how beaten down Sheri has been, she's kept Jesus and her family her center of strength.

The first time I went to see Jeff & Sheri during her battle with breast cancer; I went to their bus to visit. I'd never watched a cancer patient preparing their hair and eyebrows. I will forever cherish those few moments as we just chatted about music and family. I cry thinking what a powerful blessed woman Sheri is. As she set across the table from me, I could sense the Lord and His angels comforting and strengthening her.

Jeff & Sheri Easter and their family will forever be my FAVORITE Gospel group. I appreciate their love for one another. They are THE example of a Godly couple for us all."
Darrin Vincent, multi award-winning, Grammy-nominated blue-grass artist, Dailey & Vincent

"There could be no better title for a book by Sheri Easter than *Hear My Heart*. For more than twenty years Bill and I have had the privilege of watching this lady's heart guide her through both the painful and joyful places that inevitably come with life, parenthood, traveling, aging parents and physical battles. She has allowed Christ do in her life what He longs to do in all our lives. She has allowed Him

to define and refine her heart at every turn. We are so pleased that the world now has a chance to hear from her beautiful heart."
Gloria Gaither

"I've always been a fan of Sheri Easter, her voice and her heart. I also treasure the fact that I call her my friend. This book will allow the reader to have a glimpse of the Sheri we all know and love!"
Ivan Parker, award-winning artist

"Hear My Heart reminds us that Sheri is not only a daughter in a great family legacy, but also a daughter of God. Her willingness in sharing the fears, tears, joys and victory of her personal battle with the cancer will renew your faith. I love calling Sheri 'friend'."
Connie Hopper, award-winning artist celebrating 50 years of ministry

HEAR MY HEART

by

Sheri Easter

www.xulonpress.com

HEAR MY HEART

Sometimes I feel no one's ever been in this place before

This is hard and I'm not sure that I can do this anymore

I know someday I'll look back and all this won't seem real

But Lord right now I need you to know just how I feel

When there are no words to say and no prayer that I can pray

Hear my heart

When I don't have strength to try and I've cried all I can cry

Hear my heart

Cause you know every fear and every doubt I cannot speak

You know all the ways I need you and all the ways I'm weak

So I'll be quiet

So you can hear my heart

Every now and then I recall a simple phrase or melody

It comforts and it quiets, lifts me up and then it carries me

Far above the pain and hurt I think will never end

The song speaks words I cannot and calms the fears within

Sheri Easter/Wayne Haun/Joel Lindsey

Copyright 2009

Life is a journey—one that takes us many places and teaches us many things. Along the way, we sometimes find that we simply lose ourselves. But if we listen very closely to what our heart is saying, we can always find our way back. *Hear My Heart* is my journey through the time when I was quiet enough to listen.

I offer my heartfelt thanks to God for every opportunity, every love, and every breath. Jeff, you are and always will be the love of my life. Madison, Morgan, and Maura, you have been my greatest accomplishment. To my family and close friends, I love you and I'm so grateful for your fingerprints on my heart.

The best and most beautiful things in the world cannot be seen or even touched—they must be felt with the heart.

—Helen Keller

TABLE OF CONTENTS

Chapter One	Heart to Heart	19
Chapter Two	Queen of Hearts	31
Chapter Three	Broken Heart	41
Chapter Four	Heartfelt	52
Chapter Five	Change of Heart	61
Chapter Six	Heart's Desire	73
Chapter Seven	Have Your Heart in the Right Place	90
Chapter Eight	Absence Makes the Heart	
	Grow Fonder	106
Chapter Nine	Home Is Where the Heart Is	115
Chapter Ten	Heartache	134
Chapter Eleven	Have a Heart	158
Chapter Twelve	Know Me by Heart	167
Chapter Thirteen	Heart of the Matter	179
Chapter Fourteen	Wholehearted	197
Chapter Fifteen	Heavy Heart	205
Chapter Sixteen	Halfhearted	218
Chapter Seventeen	With All My Heart	232

CHAPTER ONE

Heart to Heart

D etermined. I've heard the story a million times. "She's breech, we'll have to turn her," the doctor told my mother. Mama recognized right away that I would be the child determined to do things her own way, a little girl with an indomitable spirit and a desire to make a difference, no matter the obstacles.

As I breathed my first breath on that Sunday afternoon in late October 1963, the South found itself gripped in hostilities brought on by racial integration while the rest of the country's free spirits experienced "enlightenment" during the Hippie generation. But tucked away in Lincolnton, Georgia, my homespun family was experiencing neither. Hardworking, God-fearing, loving, dedicated people, my family knew how to show kindness to everyone, regardless of color, and instead of choosing the road to a self-satisfying lifestyle they chose rather to live their lives outwardly in service to others.

I slipped into this world with music running through my veins. By this time Mama's family had established themselves as recording artists and performers traveling as The Lewis Family, taking their voices and instruments from one "all-day-singing-and-dinner-on-the-ground" to the next. The backdrop of country churches, picnic tables crammed with home-cooked food, talking adults, and laughing children all gathered beneath the nearest shade tree became a staple in their lives—a ritual that would mark my life years later. While Mama and her relatives sang, my daddy's family of gentle spirits worked in textile mills and served in the armed forces to make provision for those around them. Both sides shared their salt of the earth traits: good people working to make a difference.

Daddy, a simple, hardworking man who loved to fish and hunt, won perfect attendance pins year after year at the textile mill where he worked his entire life. *Field & Stream* arrived at our house every month right alongside *Better Homes and Gardens*. Mama, although she traveled and sang with her parents, brothers and sisters on weekends, would come home and assume her role as dedicated homemaker all week long. The weekends when Mama would travel, my daddy would take on the role of both parents and then arrange his swing shifts to accommodate childcare or have us stay with family or friends while he was at work.

I grew up happy. My mama's childhood nickname was Sunshine, and my daddy was so laid-back I rarely saw him move faster than a snail's pace no matter what the experience. They complemented each other in almost every way, and I never heard them argue. Everything was peaceful with my passive but outgoing Mama, and everything was agreeable with my quiet, gentle dad. They had been married for three years by the time I came along and moved into their new home (my only childhood home) the week after I was born.

Located at the foot of Graves Mountain, our house was built in a woodsy pine tree area, because my daddy loved being in the woods. It was common to see foxes, deer, raccoons, and such in our spacious backyard when I was growing up. Mama used to hang out wet laundry from a clothesline every week, and I remember watching the sheets, towels, and clothing flap in the breeze as they dried. My brother Scott and I rode our bikes in the big circular drive out front for outdoor fun.

When I was young, Lincolnton could only boast a Milky Way Freeze Bar (which is still locally owned and operated) and a couple of other local restaurants, never more than three or four. The city is comprised of an upper and lower section, and we had an "upper drugstore" and a "lower drugstore" when I was growing up.

My grandparents were an integral part of my upbringing, and I spent many days at Mama's parents' house. Both good businesswomen, my mama and grandma shared the responsibilities of running The Lewis Family office along with my aunts, Miggie and

Janis, so during most of my pre-school years and summer vacations I hung out in the office while Mama worked. By this time, The Lewis Family was traveling and singing 100,000 miles each year, performing all across the country, and had purchased their first bus, a 1948 Silverside GMC.

Spending the day with Pop meant walking in his footsteps while he carried a bucket and hoe to work in his garden. I trotted along behind him, eager to help. The strawberries didn't stand a chance when I was helping; they never made it back to the house. Most of our family meals included at least one item from Pop's garden. He brought in his daily harvest and divided it equally between any family members anxious to complete a meal with fresh fruits and vegetables.

At least once a week during the summer, he'd call everyone outside to the tiled picnic table to meet for a delicious watermelon. Sometimes, if I was lucky, I'd be down at Grandma's when it was time to use the tractor for plowing the field or bush-hogging in the late fall. Pop would let me drive the tractor while sitting in his lap, a smile stretched across my face as I steered the powerful machine across the red Georgia clay. I still love tractors today!

A few years ago, I was asked to write an article about the opening of the Southern Gospel Music Hall of Fame. Because of my family's long service to the field of Gospel music, I was honored to be a part of this historic day. I shared my thoughts about Pop and his contribution to my life as well as so many others.

The Story of Pop and Mr. Bim

I was very blessed to be brought up within two miles of my grandparents, and since my mama worked in the office every weekday, we went to work with her. We'd arrive around 10 a.m., and then it was Pop or Little Roy's turn to "take the kids and occupy them until we've finished in the office."

I had a stuffed animal, a monkey, that we named Mr. Bim. Mr. Bim was the toy of choice for me, and I played with him so often that one day at Grandma's, he lost his foot. Pop became "the doctor" and sewed Mr. Bim's foot back in place. Months later, Mr. Bim also lost an ear and was rushed back into Pop's office for another surgery. A little over forty years later, I still have Mr. Bim, and although I can't really remember any of the games I played with him, I see the stitches and I remember so vividly the care Pop gave.

When the Southern Gospel Music Hall of Fame opened in Dollywood, I proudly visited the exhibit featuring my family's memorabilia. With the banjo Little Roy learned to play was a plaque explaining that the head of the banjo had been torn and that Pop Lewis carefully stitched the head back in place. I cried. I recognized those stitches as the same handiwork that repaired my Mr. Bim. By no means were they neat or professional, but they shared the same feeling of love and dedication. Isn't it amazing whether our grandparents offer us tangible stitches or not, they somehow help hold our lives together with their touch?

On occasion, I'd spend the day washing the bus with my uncle, Little Roy. Washing the bus for me meant getting in his way while feeling like I was accomplishing much. One of my "war wound" stories occurred when I was hit in the face by the back end of a fast-paced bus brush during one of Little Roy's wash jobs. Anyone who knows him knows he does everything at lightning speed, so the injury got quite a bit of attention around our family circle, although there were no bragging rights left on my face to commemorate the day—just a tiny bruise that faded by the weekend.

My aunts, Miggie and Janis, always provided housekeeping entertainment for me. My favorite early memory of Janis is getting to "do the dishes" at her house, while Miggie's bedroom always provided enough exploration to last an entire afternoon. I'd poke through drawers and prowl the contents of her closet, turning up fascinating objects that fueled my childish imagination.

Miggie never married and so all of her attention trickled down to her brothers, sisters, nieces, and nephews. She claims she raised us all, and she's probably right. Her bedroom was decorated in the most beautiful fabrics, and at the time her bathroom was the biggest I'd ever seen, a dressing area and bath area combined. Pink tiles covered the floor and walls, and bright pink, green, and blue beads draped the doorway to separate the two rooms. Luxurious silk-covered cornice boards hung in the bedroom and bath, and everything was coordinated by the best interior decorator in a town as small as Lincolnton.

In my memories, I still think of it as one of the most beautiful places I played as a child. Her closets were full of the shiny, adorned stage dresses the girls wore for performances, and her cabinets brimmed with rhinestone jewelry to match...a little girl's heaven! I'd play dress-up for hours in her room—but of course only when I was clever enough to sneak in to play.

Recently, I wrote a piece about my childhood memories of summertime for a magazine. Funny the things you remember...

What is the goofiest thing you believed as a child? That if I dug a hole deep enough in my backyard I would dig through to hell. My friends told me not to dig too deep because if you saw the dirt turning red that meant you were getting close. In hindsight, I realize that I live in Georgia, famous for its red Georgia clay. Many times I stopped digging for fear of reaching Satan's lair.

What is one of the most embarrassing moments of your childhood? When I was young, I was very bashful and sometimes when I traveled to concerts with my family, they would always like to introduce the children. One night I remember in particular, they announced from stage that they were so happy to have Polly's daughter traveling with them and asked for me to come on stage. I was so embarrassed that I hid under the product table and wouldn't come out.

What did you tell people you wanted to be when you grew up? A singer, a secretary, and a lawyer. Most days I get to be all three!

What is one of your sweetest memories of childhood? Summertime. Because my mama handled most of the office work for the family, she would go down to my grandma's to work in the office every day for two or three hours just before lunch. While she worked I did everything from helping Pop pick strawberries, shelling butter beans, and shucking corn to riding the tractor and eating watermelon. Some days I'd help my uncle wash the bus, and other days I'd "help" with the office work by writing my name on paper at the desk with Mama. My grandma usually had a sewing project, which meant I could play with her colorful buttons. Every one of these summertime activities brings a smile to my face. It was simple. It was sweet.

Janis, the youngest of the three Lewis girls, probably took the most time caring for me since she didn't have a child of her own until nine years after I was born. She'd entertain me with her dishes, her cats, and anything that made us both laugh. I loved Janis' unbridled laughter, and I would do whatever it took to make her share it with me. By the time her baby, Lewis, was born (Janis had married and her surname was now Phillips) I had grown into a "mother" myself, taking on the nurturing of my baby brother, Scott. Since I was now an expert, Lewis became my newest fascination. I bragged for years that I changed his diapers and fed him his bottles.

My brother was born in December 1967, rounding out our family of four. Mama, under the influence of delivery drugs, said "somebody pick up all the toys," referring to the mound of toys I had pulled out just before we left for the hospital. According to relatives, Scott looked just like me, but with a more boyish face. Scott and I were always very close, and for that I am thankful. Although he was the baby of the family, I don't ever remember him being a burden to me. He was always a blessing. I loved being responsible for him and gladly accepted my role as the firstborn nurturer. Although we would fight verbally with each other, as all kids do, we were never allowed to "tussle." Our arguments were always settled with good communication skills. Not much has changed!

Mama encouraged my writing by giving me a diary, and on February 2, 1974, I made my first entry. Certainly nothing to inspire greatness, nor earth-shattering in context, it was a simple expression of a young girl trying to find her voice. Reading back over my diaries recently left me with the impression that no one should ever give a pen and paper to a thirteen-year-old. The following snippets of my life made me remember...

February 2, 1974—Today we played and had lots of fun. Karen (my first cousin) gave me a whole sack full of grape bubble gum. I chewed and chewed and chewed. But I lived. See ya! Sheri

May 16, 1977—Got my braces off.

July 18, 1977—Gospel Jubilee taping with the Hinsons.

August 8-12, 1977—My first real family vacation that I can ever remember in Fort Walton Beach, Florida.

I don't remember a lot about my daddy's parents because they died when I was young, within eleven months of each other. They lived about an hour away, and we visited every couple of months when I was small. Granddaddy was very much in stature like my daddy, tall and lean. Everyone called him Smokey Joe, and I remember vividly the yellow nicotine stains on his fingers. He always gave us a silver dollar when we visited. I still have mine. I can remember sometimes he'd slip us a 50-cent piece, but we really didn't know the difference. They were both larger than a quarter and interesting because we didn't see them often. My grandma was obviously the easiest soul to get along with as she allowed Granddaddy to paint their house hot pink! The entire exterior looked like it was coated in

Pepto-Bismol. I can't say I know many women who would give in to such an argument, but Grandma did.

I remember visiting and feeling very much at home and well loved. All of my daddy's brothers and sisters are very loving people—lots of hugging going on! These days I look so forward to their hugs.

Grandma and Granddaddy both died of heart attacks, Granddaddy in his chair and Grandma while she slept. Their funerals are the first in my memory, but what I remember most is my daddy crying. I had never seen him cry before. He loved his mother and daddy deeply. He spoke of them with so much respect in his voice. I loved the way he said "Mother." It made such a deep impact on me as a child that I still hear that tenderness today when I think of him. In November 2002, I wrote a passage for a magazine about mamas, recounting this sweet memory:

Whatever it was that she did must have been right. You could tell by the way my daddy spoke her name, "Mother." It was said with much love, devotion, respect, and honor. I don't remember much about my Grandma Williamson. She died when I was nine. I do remember her hands, however. They are my hands. Busy hands. Crafty hands. Now and again, I glance down to notice my hands and how much they look like hers.

Daddy had served in the army and was stationed in Frankfort, Germany, during his years of service. He had given my grandma and granddaddy a beautiful anniversary style clock with a glass dome covering. The clock mesmerized me as a child, one of my favorite items in Grandma's house. I didn't know until after I was married that the clock had been a gift from my daddy for his parents. My Uncle Frankie later gifted me with that clock, and I treasure the memories that it holds.

Grandma was always crocheting, knitting, or sewing. She taught my daddy a chain stitch, and he later taught me. Daddy taught me many things I wouldn't have learned otherwise, like how to shuffle cards, how to spot deer scrapings on trees, and how to recognize deer or rabbit tracks. He taught me to appreciate the outdoors, and today I can't walk a trail without thinking of my daddy.

Grandma was half Cherokee, and I remember how beautiful her olive skin looked as she sat and crocheted. Years later, Mama would tease Daddy about needing to get out in the sunshine because he was looking a little sallow. All of my daddy's siblings are so obliging, such kind, gentle spirits who love to have fun. It has become a tradition for me to host a get-together every summer for all of the Williamson family. I look so forward to this day every year. It reminds me of Daddy.

THE GIFT OF A NORMAL *Life*

Compassion®
Releasing children from poverty
in Jesus' name

When Emmanuella was a little girl, she loved to dance. She dipped and spun, watching her colorful skirt swirl around her. Over the sounds of the music, you could hear her laughter, joyful and bright.

But as Emmanuella grew older, the sound of her laughter was replaced with a rattled breathing in her throat. She grew tired more easily and had a hard time keeping up with her friends. It wasn't long before there were no more twirling skirts — only lethargy and weakness.

While her mother, Hannah, noticed the change in Emmanuella, she was unable to afford the costs of a diagnosis.

"I saw that she could not do any activity without getting tired," says Hannah. "She could not live a normal life like her older brother. She isolated herself when other children were running around and playing."

[over, please]

Partners of Compassion *Highlights* . . .

Between January 1 and March 31, 2013 . . .

$1.7 million
was used to support *highly vulnerable children*

$3.5 million
went to care for children's *medical needs*

$33,000
was used for *educational support*

PARTNERS OF
Compassion

CHAPTER TWO

Queen of Hearts

My preschool and elementary school years were pretty much like everyone else's I assume. They accused me of attending kindergarten twice because the lady who babysat us on weekends had two great granddaughters, one my age and one a year older. Big Mama was all about being fair. If one child did it, all the children did it. I never remember feeling like I wasn't a part of her family because she treated Scott and me just like her own. So when the oldest great granddaughter, Dawn, started kindergarten, Dana and I begged to go. The tiny one-room school housed only a few preschoolers, so it didn't seem like a burden to Mrs. Vera that she had two "extras" most days. The next year Dana and I enrolled for our official year of kindergarten, and I loved every moment of both terms.

Big Mama and Mrs. Vera were such wonderful inspirations to me in my early years. My little brother, Scott, was named after Big Mama, Fannie Mae Scott, and Mrs. Vera Burton taught the kindergarten in a small building beside her home. They made me feel very special, which is just the thing that every child needs to know. I was blessed to have such caring teachers throughout my early childhood, another great quality of living in a small town where everybody knows everybody. They all knew my family and loved me through any of the days Mama had to be away. I remember Mrs. Mildred Fortson, one of my elementary school teachers, would let me sit on her lap during many of my classes. Years later, after I was married, she told me she went the extra mile because she could tell when my mama had to be away. Funny, I never remember it bothering me, but she always knew. To this day, I have a fondness for teachers.

Though I loved singing, I was such a bashful child I couldn't conceive of doing it onstage in front of people. I would have been happy to sing in my bedroom behind a closed door, but that's not how singers make a living, which is one of the reasons I wondered if it would ever be my career.

I sang all the time—in my room, on the hearth in the den, at the kitchen table (of course, I was reprimanded), but I never sang in front of anyone. The thought of standing and looking into someone's eyes while I shared my heart with them was much too scary.

My little brother and I were close in age with our cousins who lived beside us. As we got older, we began staying with my aunt during the weekends while Mama was traveling. My cousin Karen and I both loved to sing, and we entertained many times from the top of their backyard picnic table to an audience of none! We would carry my daddy's battery-operated turntable outside and play Donny & Marie Osmond records and sing along. I usually sang Donny's part because my voice was lower.

Every week Daddy would give me an allowance of one dollar to go with my cousins on their grocery trip, and almost every week I spent my one dollar on a 45rpm single. I bought everything from The Osborne Brothers' "Rocky Top" to Grand Funk Railroad's "Locomotion." I bought a lot of male singers and also Rita Coolidge because she sang in my key. Most of the well-known female voices were much too high for me to sing along. We'd bring the singles home and play songs, performing atop the picnic table until dark, when the lightning bugs would come out, their tiny lights flickering across the yard.

A List of Me

We are a great compilation of stories, happy and sad, good and bad; nevertheless a complex structure of what life has made us. These are a few of the things that have made me:

Music

Prayer

Good parents, grandparents, and a close-knit family

Rural life

Hope

A piano

Laughter and tears, I needed them both

Shelling purple hull peas

Lightning bugs and big black grasshoppers

Best friends

Front porch rockers and swings

Spankings

Fishing

Faith

Shucking corn, brushing the silks in a basket

Dance

The lyrics in a song, the words in a book

4-H and other clubs for young people

Love

Picking strawberries

Washing dishes

Xxx's and Ooo's

Paperwork, real and make-believe

Jeff, Madison, Morgan, and Maura…you have not only made me, but made me complete!

It was my aunt Janis and my mama who first taught me how to sing harmony. As we rode along in the bus one weekend I expressed an interest in learning. They demonstrated on the song "Little Brown Church in the Wildwood." Every time I hear that song I think of singing the alto part over and over until I got it right.

One of the funniest stories I remember from my childhood involves cleaning out the gerbil cage with a vacuum cleaner! My brother and I each had a gerbil, a little hamster- like pet. I'm such a perfectionist, and I've never counted patience as one of my virtues, so when my mama asked me to clean out the gerbil cage, I figured the vacuum cleaner would get the job done best in the quickest amount of time. I was about 12 years old and never considered what the outcome might be! As soon as the tiny creature came in contact with the powerful vacuum, it sucked him in. I panicked and grabbed him by the tail, never considering turning off the power. Within seconds, I had only a tail in my hand, screaming for Mama and when she quickly assessed the situation, she turned off the vacuum cleaner and began to laugh hysterically. Looking back, I agree it must have been a ridiculous sight—me with a vacuum cleaner hose in one hand and a gerbil tail in the other.

By this time, I was crying uncontrollably and Mama was separating the hose connections trying to locate the little guy. About that time, he slowly backed out of one of the hoses and appeared fine. Daddy called the vet and was told to clip the bone and put Merthiolate on the tip end of the stumped tail. My little gerbil lived another seven years, and from that time on we never had trouble confusing my gerbil from my brother's.

By the time I reached my freshman year of high school, I had become the person I am now, volunteering for everything, enrolling in every class, joining every club, and seeking out ways to be a part of everything for which I'm qualified. I didn't want to miss a thing—sign me up! I was a member of National Honor Society, Debate Team, Co-Y, Future Business Leaders of America, 4-H, Student Council, and the list goes on. I participated in beauty pageants, volunteered to take goody baskets to the senior citizens, and acted as a junior leader for the younger club member activities. I was nominated for Homecoming Court in my ninth grade year. I never realized how such a simple activity could change my life so drastically. After the nomination, I couldn't wait to represent my class for Homecoming, until I found out that to compete you had to perform a talent. My initial thought was, *Oh my, I can't twirl a baton, I can't dance, I can't play piano...I don't have a talent. I guess I'll have to sing!*

The thought of it scared me to death, but God has a perfect timing, and for me the timing was now. One of my best friends was also one of the best singers I've ever heard, even now. Reese LeRoy had the warmest, richest baritone and knew how to sing from his heart. He and I had spent a lot time together because of our love of gospel music. I asked him if he'd help me because I had an idea for a three-minute musical I could sing and act out based on the Elvis movie *Frankie and Johnny*. He agreed.

I loved old Elvis movies. Staying at home on the weekends with my daddy gave me lots of time to watch the old classic movies, everything from Humphrey Bogart to John Wayne, but my favorite was Elvis. I had the idea that I could sing the title song and dress up to be Frankie. I started creating with the help of Lonnie Martin, the most gifted set designer in the county of Lincoln; Denise Biggerstaff, who had the coolest black-and-white shimmy style costume; and Reese, who played the piano for me, gave me moral support, and played the part of Johnny. I worked on the performance for weeks, creating entrances, how to play each verse and chorus as a different scene, and whatever I could do to make it exciting! Because my daddy loved hunting, he had a large gun collection. The only one ever kept in our house was a blank gun, a cute little thing that would fit perfectly in a garter in a scene from a movie set in a saloon—I had found my exciting finale!

The day of the performance, I stepped onstage, walked through a cascade of silver garland, and started to sing. I sang with passion. I sang with attitude. I sang believing that my hard work would finally pay off. For the final line of the song, I mourned "But he done me wrong" and turned to shoot the blank gun as "Johnny" slumped over the keys of a piano. The auditorium erupted in applause and I was never the same. I had performed with everything I had to give, and it was good. I never looked back from that moment on. I knew the stage was where I was supposed to be. I would have to trust God to give me the ability to walk out on stage for every performance from that day on. In my weakness, He is made strong—when I can't, He can. It's about knowing your limitations and trusting that God can make all the difference when you give everything to Him. On Friday night, during the half-time show, with the bass drums beating and the crowd cheering, I took my daddy's arm and walked out onto the field to be crowned Homecoming Queen 1979-80.

After that first performance, other events came along in quick succession.

March 13, 1980—Miss Lincoln County Green pageant, first runner-up.

April 4, 1980—Sang Mama's part with The Lewis Family while Mama recovered from surgery.

August 1980—Won Miss Georgia Teen, Talent Division

January 1981—Won Miss LCHS (Lincoln County High School)

My high school years are some of my fondest memories. I had wonderful friends, I loved my classes and my teachers, and I loved being busy. Although I concentrated on most of the business classes, I also loved English Literature. Math was never my strongest subject, but I enjoyed the challenge, and because of my teacher I loved all of my high school sciences.

During my senior year I took a job with my great uncle as a receptionist and bookkeeper for his poultry company for a half-day every weekday. I loved the responsibility, all the while gaining school credit for my business class. It gave me a sense of accomplishment and fulfillment, knowing that I was able to help someone by giving of my time. Plus, it gave me some spending money for a trip to the mall every now and then.

Mama never missed any of the family's concerts except due to childbirth twice, surgery once, and a broken leg. When I found out the date scheduled for my graduation, we realized she was booked in Canada the following day and that it would be impossible for the family to leave after graduation and still make the date. At that point, my mama made the greatest sacrifice I ever remember. She is a worrier and had never flown anytime or anywhere. She and my little brother, Scott, flew to Canada for the concert after my graduation. None of us ever dreamed she could do it! I'm so grateful that she did.

My prom, football games, and senior assemblies were all very special, and my time at Lincoln County High School was nearing its end. For our baccalaureate service, my classmates and I sang Bill Gaither's "Because He Lives." I was excited for my future but nostalgic about my past. For our senior superlatives, my classmates voted me as Best All Around, and I graduated with honors in the Class of 1981.

Don't cry over anything that can't cry over you.

—My Daddy

CHAPTER THREE

Broken Heart

I grew up thinking I was a princess, with a wonderful family and so many good friends who loved me. My bedroom was decorated in dusty blue and white-flocked wallpaper. White furnishings and a canopy bed draped in a sheer blue voile fabric completed the look, with dolls and stuffed animals everywhere. I had only experienced death when I was young enough not to fully understand, and no one I knew personally had ever divorced. My life was perfect and free from real pain until my third year in college.

Ever since my freshman year in high school I knew I would become a Dawg. Athens and the University of Georgia were only an hour from my house, and I always wanted to attend college there. I loved the stately oak trees and redbrick walkways that meandered throughout the campus, with massive colonial-style buildings. I also loved anything to do with business and enrolled in whatever classes

I needed to earn a business degree. Suddenly, at age seventeen, I found myself in a world that was one hundred times larger than the one in which I had grown up. I like familiarity, so I spent the next four years walking the same routes, eating in the same restaurants, and doing a lot of the same routines—wake up, go to class, eat a pack of cheese crackers and a Tab for lunch, study in the library, stop by the local gyro shop for my regular sandwich, and then head home. Of course, after the first year work was thrown into the mix, but you get the idea.

As much as I loved Athens, I loved home more, so every weekend as soon as classes ended I'd drive home either to travel with my family if the schedule allowed or to stay home with my daddy. The weekends were my time of restoration—time to get ready for the routine again. But by the time the weekend was over, I was anxious to get back to school. I was a serious student and loved to learn, but every now and then I wondered if I was where God wanted me to be. It was hard, but I loved a challenge. Mama used to tell everyone that I quit school twice—my freshman year and my junior year—but I never notified the school! I guess that's right; my heart gave up a time or two, but my driven personality wouldn't allow me to quit. I jotted the following entries in my journal:

September 1981—Started college at the University of Georgia, Athens, Georgia. I'm living in the dorm.

January 1982—Moved into my first apartment.

By the end of my junior year, I was solidly on my way to obtaining my Bachelor of Business Administration degree in marketing. I was twenty years old and loving life. After taking my final exam I called Mama to tell her I was on my way home. We talked several times a day, and it was our practice to contact each other just before I left so she would know I was all right and on time. My mama was a talker, and even a quick "out-the-door" call usually took several minutes, but this call was different. At the time, I wasn't sure what that meant. I simply noticed it was different.

"Hey, Mama, I'm on my way," I said as soon as she picked up the phone. "Okay, Sheri, drive carefully," she replied and hung up. It was so abrupt it bordered on rude, but because my mama has never been rude, that didn't seem like a possibility. Oh well, I'd be home in an hour and she could explain. I packed up the car and started the drive to Lincolnton. Just as I crossed the Lincoln County line, a state trooper pulled in behind me and motioned for me to pull over to the side of the road. I panicked. I wasn't doing anything wrong and couldn't have been speeding because I had just looked at the speedometer.

When he walked up, I recognized his face immediately. The officer was from Lincolnton, a friend of our family and the first officer who ever gave me a speeding ticket. As soon as I saw him I smiled. He continued up to the car and asked me how I was doing.

Fine. Are you still at UGA? Yes sir. It's good to see you. You too. Have a good day! Okay. And I drove away with a *that's so weird I can't wait to tell Daddy* thought in my head. Five minutes later, I pulled into our drive.

It was the Tuesday before Father's Day, and I had cross-stitched my daddy a coffee mug that read "Anyone can be a Father, but it takes someone special to be a Daddy." I shoved it deep into my bag so that I could walk quickly past my daddy without it being spotted. He would be in his recliner, for that was the only place he ever was while he was at home. As I opened the door, Mama said, "Sheri, Elzie had a heart attack and he's dead." My head whirled, my knees buckled, and I dropped to the floor in uncontrollable sobs. The words didn't make any sense. How could it be? Not *my* daddy. I stood and faced a room full of friends and family, and my eyes searched them all for my daddy. Where was my daddy? I don't remember much after that, but Mama calmed me down and explained how everything had happened.

Years later, our friend the state trooper told me he had followed me home. Prior to stopping me, he had learned of my daddy's death and was making sure I was okay to drive. He told me as soon as he saw my smile that afternoon he knew I was unaware of the horrible news that awaited me.

Daddy had worked the night shift at the mill, and when he came home he had breakfast and headed for bed. Mama was getting ready in the bathroom that adjoined their bedroom, and she heard a sound, a gurgle. When she reached him, he was holding his chest, unable to speak. She called for an ambulance, and the local doctor in our town also responded. They worked with him for over an hour but couldn't revive him. He was gone. This all happened an hour or so before I got home. My mama said that's why she couldn't speak to me when I called. She was so afraid I would hear it in her voice, and she didn't want to let me find out that way knowing I had a drive ahead of me.

The next few hours went by in a blur except for one thing. I vividly remember going to the funeral home to make the arrangements. They carried us into a room filled with caskets, and I fell apart again. I just couldn't choose one of these to put my sweet Daddy in. The thought of his precious body being sealed in a casket and vault and put in the ground just crushed me. Scott, who was sixteen at the time, appeared to be handling it pretty well, but I knew he was broken too. We stood there, the funeral director, Mama, my brother, and me, and together we selected a beautiful steel gray casket because it matched Daddy's hair and the only suit he owned, the gray suit he had worn five years earlier when he walked me onto the field to be crowned homecoming queen.

He was buried on Wednesday because all of our friends and family had arrived and there was no reason to wait. Every detail had been attended to. I don't remember all the people, but there were many. I do remember the flowers—so many, many flowers. And I remember the casket being closed and carried out by pallbearers. I wanted to scream for them to stop and let me see him once more, but I didn't. I sobbed, knowing that my last time to ever see Daddy's face had passed and there was nothing I could do about it.

My journal entries from that time capture my thoughts and feelings about my daddy's sudden death:

June 12, 1984—Came home from Athens. Daddy died today of a heart attack. Many people came, all of Daddy and Mama's family. Daddy looked so good. He had on his gray suit. He looked so beautiful, as if he were asleep. So many people came. I didn't get to give him his Father's Day gift, his cup. I love you, Daddy.

June 13, 1984—I slept with Mama last night. We didn't sleep much! We all went to see Daddy this morning. It hurt so much to leave him. There were so many people and so many flowers. We had the funeral at 4 p.m. He was buried in a pretty spot. Scott's [my brother] terrific. He's so strong.

July 16, 1984—Man came today about tombstones. We picked out a beautiful one!

For several days, I drove to the grave to just sit alone and cry. Why did God have to take my daddy so soon? I let the tears stream down my face as I talked to God. One day as I was praying I came to a realization that forever changed my relationship with Him. It solidified the relationship and became a foundation for me to build upon. Here are my thoughts that I later wrote in a magazine article.

One of my darkest moments came when I was only twenty years old and my Daddy died suddenly of a heart attack. I had been so blessed to have a close and loving family that we were stunned by the tragedy. I sought God for answers to the toughest questions I had ever asked of Him. Why? I simply didn't understand, but I had been taught to revere God and didn't feel that I had the right to question His will. I was at the gravesite alone, crying and praying. I remember saying, "God, it's just that I'm so…ANGRY!" I gritted my teeth and yelled the word, and slowly opened my eyes, expecting to feel the wrath of God. Instead, all was quiet. Tears flooded my face as I realized that God wasn't challenged by my questions, nor was He intimidated or surprised by my anger. I had doubted His unconditional love, assuming that if I lashed out in anger, it would result in Him no longer loving me. I am grateful that from that day forward, the limitless love of God has filled my life, and the honesty of my heart is safe with Him.

In every thing give thanks: for this is the will of
God in Christ Jesus concerning you.

1 Thessalonians 5:18 (KJV)

Several years after my daddy died, I heard a preacher preach a message on "In everything, give thanks." By this time I was comfortable asking God questions, and I prayed asking Him how I could give thanks for my daddy's death. Immediately, that still small voice said, "Sheri, you can be grateful you had a *good* daddy for twenty years. Many aren't so fortunate." I have been able to affirm that scripture at many other times in my life by keeping the right perspective.

When someone dies, we have to find ways to continue breathing in and breathing out, and several circumstances helped me to cope. First was the realization that my life had changed and that I would have to learn to live without my daddy. It was as though I had been acting in a play when all of a sudden the curtains closed, the play ended, the set was scratched, and we were no longer our character but another new character in another new play. It took a lot of adjusting. I became Mama's partner in all of her decision-making, and she became more than my mama; she became my closest friend and confidante.

Second, I searched the Bible and other books on grief hoping that my healing would come through words. I read through the Psalms many times, relating to the anguish that David felt. I memorized many of the Scriptures and quoted them to myself over and over. I found a beautiful poem on a sympathy card that read,

My life is but a weaving, between my God and me.

I do not choose the colors, He worketh steadily.

Oftimes, He weaveth sorry, and I in foolish pride,

Forget He sees the upper and I the underside.

Not till the loom is silent and shuttles cease to fly,

Will God unroll the canvas and explain the reason why.

The dark threads are as needed in the skillful weaver's hand

As the threads of gold and silver in the pattern He has planned.

—Grant Colfax Tuller

I not only read this poem, I memorized it; I cross-stitched it and hung it in my room, and I quoted it back to myself every time I felt that life was unfair.

Thirdly, I believe in a God who is intimate, who hears my prayers and is concerned for even the smallest of my needs. I had a dream one night about a year after my daddy died. He walked toward me and then I woke up. It lasted only a matter of seconds, and to anyone else it may not have appeared significant in any way, but to me it was a glimpse into heaven. My daddy had a severe deterioration in his lower back, and for all of my childhood he walked with a limp. I had never seen him walk without it...until the dream.

But they that wait upon the LORD shall renew their
strength; they shall mount up with wings as eagles;
they shall run, and not be weary; and they
shall walk, and not faint.

Isaiah 40:31 (KJV)

CHAPTER FOUR

Heartfelt

I performed professionally for the first time in 1980 when Mama had to be off the road for six weeks to recover from surgery. During my latter years of high school and all four years of college, I would travel with my family and sing. Singing had become such a huge part of my life by this time. I had won the talent competition for the Miss Georgia Teen pageant, and I loved the outlet that music provided for me. As a young adult, I made many sacrifices to be able to travel. I forfeited football games, movies, and the other typical teen activities. I remember asking a friend for advice regarding traveling and singing or staying home and doing the things I loved there. He looked at me as though I were crazy and went on to explain why the answer was so obvious to him. After much prayer and wrestling with what I should do, I finally made peace with my decision. I gave up my position in church as a part of the music ministry team and

Sunday school teacher. I knew I was doing what God had gifted me to do, and I was happy.

It had been a very difficult few weeks since Daddy's death, and I was just beginning to heal when I performed at a concert in August 1984 at the Albert E. Brumley memorial singing in Springdale, Arkansas. Throughout my youth I had been very blessed to date some really special guys, but by this time I had begun to think it would be a while before I considered marriage; the traveling took so much of my time that a serious relationship didn't seem feasible.

As I was standing backstage, I saw a very handsome man who immediately stole my attention. He had dark hair, eyes that sparkled, and a beautiful, comfortable smile. He was wearing a pale pink jacket and was just about the cutest thing I'd ever seen. I nudged my mama and said, "Don't look now, but who's the guy in the pink jacket?" She looked. He caught us looking and headed over to introduce himself. "Hey, Polly, do you remember me?"

Mama apologized, "I'm not sure I do." "I'm Jeff Easter, James Easter of The Easter Brothers' son. My family wrote 'They're Holding Up the Ladder,' and I was the one who gave it to y'all on the way to the recording," Jeff explained. Immediately, my mama said, "Yes, Jeff, it's nice to see you. This is my daughter Sheri."

We spent the entire concert talking about life and death. I poured out my soul to him over my daddy's death, and he offered wonderful, humorous stories that made me laugh even though it would have been easy to cry. Everything about him was comfortable to me—his laugh, his mannerisms, and especially his stories. He had been brought up in a bluegrass gospel singing family just like mine. We tease now because that first glimpse of him was so consuming that I never realized he was walking with someone. I later learned that someone was Michael English, who has always been a very handsome man, but in all honesty I never noticed. I saw only Jeff Easter. Later that night on the bus, my mama and aunts asked me what I thought of him. "I'm picking out my china pattern!" was all I could say.

I had given Jeff an 8x10 publicity photo of me, and he put it up on The Singing Americans' bus in the room he shared with Michael. "She's way out of your league, buddy," Michael teased. Jeff was telling this story on a recent video, and Michael added, "She's still out of your league."

August 4, 1984—Springdale, AR. Met Jeff Easter with Singing Americans.

September 6, 1984—Daddy's grave marker will be placed today.

I'm not sure why we didn't exchange numbers that night, but Jeff and I didn't hear from each other until about six weeks later at the National Quartet Convention in Nashville. I went hoping I'd run into him, and at the softball game between the different artists

I spotted him but never went up to speak. By the time I saw him again, his group was leaving for their next concert and we had only a quick "hello and goodbye" as they left the venue. Still we hadn't exchanged information, and again we separated with no intentions of communicating—until a month later.

I was scheduled for exams and wasn't able to travel with my family to the annual peanut festival in Dothan, Alabama. Multiple groups performing for concerts aren't always aware of the other groups who are also scheduled to perform, and I had no idea The Singing Americans were on the same bill as my family that weekend. As soon as my mama saw Jeff, he asked about me. To which Mama replied, "She just broke up with her boyfriend. You should call her sometime." Within minutes Jeff called me, and since that day we haven't missed a day talking to each other.

Conversation came easily with Jeff, and he was so comfortable in his own skin that he made me feel like I was a longtime friend. We had so much in common that we could talk for hours and never have a loss for words. We knew many of the same people, loved a lot of the same music, and had both been brought up in gospel music families. He told me he'd be performing the next night in Georgia and if it was close enough, maybe I could come to see him. It was close enough—anywhere within driving distance would have been close enough!

That next morning I woke up with birds singing, sunshine warming my skin, and a sweet aroma in the air. I'm not sure if all of this was actual, but it sure felt that way in my head! I went to classes and then to my job as an interviewer for the Unemployment Claims office. I loved my job and the people I worked with. Giddy with excitement, I explained to my co-workers that Jeff was a couple of hours away and that I wanted to see him, but I wasn't sure if I had enough gas to get there and back. One of my co-workers filled my tank, and another offered me a $20 loan. They must have known I was serious!

I drove to a church in Rockmart, Georgia, and arrived about ten minutes before the concert started so I didn't get to see Jeff before the performance. I did notice there was a steel guitarist who looked a lot like Jeff, and I assumed it must be his brother "Rabbit." Sure enough, Steve was sitting in with the guys that night. After the concert, Jeff invited me to go to Waffle House with them. Before we could begin a conversation, one of his friends walked up and said, "Have you told her about the ex-wife and kids yet?" I laughed. Jeff didn't. Uh-oh, did I miss something?

Jeff explained that he had met someone when he was eighteen and married her within two weeks. Two children and three years later, she filed for divorce. I listened carefully and searched his face for the things he might not have been able to put into words. We had a wonderful time, but I left so confused. I remember praying, "God, what are You doing? Of all the guys I've dated, I've never been more sure, but he's divorced and has two children. What does this mean? Is my heart mistaken?"

I headed home and talked with Mama. She was always such a good sounding board and always had the right answers. Was I supposed to let this one go because of a mistake in his past, when everything else about him was perfect for me? This time she simply told me, "Only you will know."

I had been brought up in a godly home, involved heavily in my local church, and I didn't know anyone personally who had ever been divorced. What did this mean? What should I do? I began searching the Scriptures just as I had after Daddy's death. After a few days, I prayed and asked God to take away any feelings I had for Jeff or else change my perspective about a divorced man. Maybe a good man can be involved in a marriage that fails? What about the children? Am I ready for this?

Jeff and I continued to talk all during this time, and I'm sure I asked a million questions. What are the children's names? Ages? What do they look like? Why did the marriage end? How long has it been? Jeff was so open and offered every detail. He asked if I'd like to meet his kids? Sure, why not!

By November of that year, I took my first trip to Mount Airy, North Carolina, where I met Jeff's daddy, his mama, his sister Teresa, and Misty and Josh, his five-year-old daughter and four-year-old son. They were beautiful...big blue eyes and sandy blonde hair! Both were very sweet, and I knew immediately that they had my heart.

In December, after we had celebrated with my family, Jeff and I went back up to his hometown for Christmas. We carried gifts and celebrated with his family. After the celebration, he told me we needed to drive up the mountain so he could pick up my gift. He left me at a friend's house while he "went to the store." When he returned, we headed back down the mountain without a word about the gift. I asked him if he had gotten what he wanted. (Yes, he did.) I asked him where it was. (It was in the glove compartment.) I asked him if I could have it. (Of course.) He pushed play on the cassette, and Kenny Rogers and Dolly Parton began to sing "Knowing you're in love with me is the greatest gift of all." I opened the box, and in it was the most beautiful engagement ring I had ever seen. I said yes.

Reading through the journal entries of those days takes me back, helping to recapture the thoughts and feelings of being a young woman about to marry the man she loves.

December 21, 1984—Jeff gave me an engagement ring.

January 4, 1985—Mama and I went to Athens (Georgia) to the bridal shop. I bought my dress, veil, shoes, and hose and got a garter free!

June 18, 1985—Our wedding!

I was finishing up my last semester of college and planning my wedding at the same time. I received my BBA in marketing and continued working part-time at the Georgia Department of Labor and part-time with The Lewis Family. Jeff was traveling with The Singing Americans. We were usually together all week and then separated for the weekend for our concerts. I planned our wedding for June 18, 1985, the week after the first anniversary of my daddy's death, so that I would have something to celebrate instead of something to lament.

I chose the song "To Me" for us to sing to each other because of the line that says, "Just as sure as I'm sure there's a heaven, this was meant to be," because after ten months of prayer and getting to know Jeff and his family, I was sure. Michael English sang our favorite song, "You're the Inspiration." It was a beautiful celebration with family and friends. My sweet little brother offered my hand in marriage "in memory of our father."

One week later, The Singing Americans replaced Jeff with another employee who had filled in during our honeymoon. After one week of marriage, Jeff was unemployed. He called my mama, who asked him not to tell me until she could make a few calls. By the time he and Mama called me, The Lewis Family had hired their first piano and harmonica player, their first employee who was not a blood relative. It was evident that God was continuing His work in our lives.

July 1, 1985 — Jeff called Mama. Lewis Family hired him.

July 9, 1985 — Cooked Jeff his first supper. (Keep in mind, my mama was a recent widow and loved preparing meals for us. This, in addition to our hectic summer touring schedule, is the only defense I can offer as to why it took almost a month for me to cook him supper.)

CHAPTER FIVE

Change of Heart

J ust after our wedding, Jeff played a copy of the song we sang to each other to then president of Riversong Records, Bill Traylor. Bill told Jeff if we ever decided we wanted to do a project to call him. A few months after we married, we called Bill and began selecting songs for what would be our first recording together.

Recording a project is so much more than most people realize. It accounts for about a year of your life, listening and living with hundreds of songs until you finally reduce that number to ten. Then there are the months of scheduling musicians, arranging and rehearsing songs, researching copyright information, writing charts and liners, and finally the day of the session arrives.

Our first tracking session was scheduled for Martin Luther King's birthday in 1987. We worked hand-in-hand with friend, gentleman, and master fiddler Buddy Spicher. He not only led us through every stage of the preparation process but also had us in his home while we rehearsed. The record company didn't have any artists quite like us and wondered if we were capable of producing our own project. We had never done anything like it, but that had never stopped us before. We set out to record the best quality project we could, never knowing if we would ever get another opportunity like this. To this day, we are still proud of and love *A New Tradition*. I tell young artists all the time to make certain the projects you record are the very best you can do. They live on forever.

A New Tradition was just who we are, musically, emotionally, spiritually. It included songs about heaven, songs that encouraged in the here and now, and songs about the love between a husband and wife, something slightly unconventional for a gospel music project. Then again, we weren't your ordinary artists. We were a couple of young newlyweds in love who had been given an unbelievable opportunity to produce their own project and record for one of gospel music's most respected labels. We were blessed.

We didn't know if we would ever again have the chance to record, so we did everything first rate. We hired a list of Nashville's greatest musicians, spending more money on the tracking session alone than some would spend on an entire project. We were frugal and knew that we would have to cut corners elsewhere to stay within budget. By producing ourselves, we didn't have the expense of hiring a producer, so we used the entire budget on getting the best record we could. We chose songs that spoke to us spiritually and felt it was a part of our ministry to record love songs to encourage other young marrieds like ourselves. Perfectionists, we critiqued our performances giving 150 percent in everything we did.

Jeff and I spent the week working nonstop from 10 a.m. to 2 a.m. every day for five days, with the final day ending at 5 a.m. We got in our car and started the six-hour drive home to Lincolnton, listening to *A New Tradition* the entire way. We got home just in time to get on the bus and leave for The Lewis Family's weekend of touring.

Those were wonderful, hectic days, and my journal entries give a snapshot of what it was like to record our first album:

November 19, 1986 — Met Norman to sign (recording) contract (with Riversong Records). Called musicians to book them for our sessions. Pictures are to be made December 9. Album to be recorded January 19-23. Got back to Lincolnton around 11:30 p.m. Bought Amy Grant's book with my picture in it. (This was such a cool moment for me because I was a new artist and this book was everywhere! I had met Amy at a Word picnic in the spring of 1984, and she and I, along with pals Kelly Nelon and Tanya Goodman, had a photo op together.)

January 19, 1987 — To Nashville to record our album. Sessions began at 2:00 p.m. Musicians were all there and

everything sounded great. Mama and Travis got in around
6:00 p.m.

March 25, 1987—Got our first copies of our album.

Our first review in *Singing News* magazine was a five-star review
with the statement that until that time no project had ever received
five stars because there was no such thing as a perfect album. I'm
paraphrasing, but our now longtime friend Jerry Kirksey wrote that
it was a perfect album because it was just the right artists, with all
the right songs, and all the right music—a perfect combination. We
were so excited we collected several copies of the magazine and put
them in our cedar chest for nostalgia's sake. Our first single was a
remake of an old Louvin Brothers song, "There's a Higher Power,"
and it charted as high as number 6 in the national charts.

We continued to travel with my family and were so blessed to
have a platform to promote our music. Jeff played piano and harmonica, helped set up equipment, ran sound, and sang harmonies
while I sang harmonies and performed a feature song for each set.
We were doing what we loved, and I had the added bonus of doing
it beside my mama. I loved the melding of our voices. There really
is something very special about family harmony.

Jeff played on his first recording when he was thirteen years old.
The Easter Brothers recorded a project called *He's Everything I Need*
and asked Jeff to play bass as they were about to leave to record. The

scheduled bass player had cancelled and they were in need of a fast replacement. From that time, Jeff played with his family for several years, finally leaving home and taking his first job away from the family in 1980 to play bass for Gold City. He was there about a year and then moved back to Mount Airy. It was during this time that his marriage was ending, and as much as he tried, he couldn't find solid ground. He says that Tim Riley helped him so much in the year he lived in Dahlonega, Georgia, by offering sound advice and a listening ear. Jeff is still very close to Tim because of his kindness. He returned home to play once again for his family and in 1984 took a job with The Singing Americans.

During our travels with my family, we began to gain attention, winning awards in bluegrass music. I won my first professional award in 1986 as Female Vocalist-Contemporary by the Society for the Preservation of Bluegrass Music Association. Mama won Female Vocalist-Traditional that same year, while my family won several other awards from Traditional Group of the Year to Entertainer of the Year for my uncle, Little Roy.

Jeff and I both come from families who love to laugh! His family is more of the comedic, storytelling kind of funny, while my family oozes with dry wit and sarcasm. Needless to say, we can always find something to laugh about. Our favorite family characters who keep us laughing are my Aunt Miggie and Jeff's Uncle Edd. Miggie is the "old maid" sister as Little Roy likes to joke about, and she's forever doing or saying something funny.

One of my favorite Miggie stories took place back in the day of person-to-person phone calls. Calling long distance was expensive, and so everyone devised ways of getting around paying the price if they could. To place a person-to-person call, you would tell the operator that you were calling for "John Smith." If John Smith wasn't available, the operator would inform you and you wouldn't be charged. The record company was expecting product to arrive for the family, and they would be stopping by Nashville to pick it up on their way through. If the product arrived, they agreed that the company president would call person-to-person for himself, The Lewis Family would say he's not available, and they would know the product had arrived and was ready to be picked up.

Miggie usually answered the calls that came into the office but was caught off guard when the operator asked for John Smith. Miggie began stammering around with questions and comments and then remembered "the code." Immediately, she told the operator, "Oh, oh, okay, all right, I understand," then hung up!

Another classic Miggie moment was the day she brought in an envelope holding it away from her body, pinching it with two fingers as though it were contaminated. She handed the letter to my mama, who was slightly aggravated at the drama surrounding the note. Mama said, "Miggie, what's wrong, why are you being so silly?" Miggie replied, "I don't want to catch anything. It says she has hepatitis!" Upon reading the note, Mama corrected, "Miggie, it does NOT say she has hepatitis, it says she had a HYSTERECTOMY!"

Jeff's uncle Edd is equally funny and called the brothers once, saying he had wrecked into a bank on his way to the bus. Jeff headed up the mountain looking over every embankment the whole way. He stopped at the first pay phone he found to tell the other family members he couldn't find Edd anywhere. They explained, "While you were gone, Edd called back and clarified that he didn't run into *a* bank, he ran into THE FIRST NATIONAL BANK." Jeff turned around slowly, and sure enough there was Edd's car and the bank!

Laughter has carried us through many difficult days, and come to think of it, it's made the good days even better. Below is an article I wrote concerning the importance of a smile:

A writer can only write what is inside. Many times I've wondered whether I had anything of value to say to a reader, however, the desire to write has never weakened or diminished. It grows stronger with each opportunity I postpone; therefore, I picked up a pen and began to jot down things that were in my heart. My prayer is that someone can take with them a similar memory, story, or quote and find comfort in the words—the kind of comfort that brings a smile. "Open up your heart and let the sun shine in"…barely able to talk, but boastfully proud to sing, I was about three or four years old when my mama taught me the words to this song. I'd sing as loud as I could into my jump rope, standing on "stage" on the fireplace hearth, bellowing out the message of a smile.

My mama preached smiling and reinforced her sermon with action. She smiled through it all—business struggles, family squabbles, and even sickness and death, somehow Polly could find a smile. Don't get me wrong, it wasn't the "smile on your face, frown in your heart" kind of smile. It was a genuine joy, a "we have to smile to survive" kind of smile. It's been proven that it takes more muscles to frown than to smile and that laughter is good like a medicine. Mama believed those adages and taught them with great conviction. It's a lesson I learned and respected early on, and I try daily to teach it to my children. Life can be overwhelming, but it sure helps to smile!

Jeff and I were so fortunate to be able to travel together working with many of our musical heroes from our childhood, from The Osborne Brothers, Howard and Vestal Goodman, Bill Monroe, Jake Hess, Ralph Stanley, Lester Flatt & Earl Scruggs to George Jones and Tammy Wynette. We also worked with many newcomers like us who eventually became artists recognized the world over, people such as Marty Stuart; Rhonda Vincent, Darrin Vincent, and Jaime Dailey of Dailey & Vincent; Allison Krauss; Jerry Douglas; and Marty Rabon. We sang at the Ryman Auditorium, the Grand Ole

Opry, The Smithsonian Institute, and many other famous auditoriums and arenas.

We recorded our second project, *Homefolks*, and also recorded three projects with The Lewis Family featuring us on one or two songs per project. We both were brought up in bluegrass music and loved the close harmonies and haunting melodies, yet we enjoyed other genres as well, adding piano, steel guitar, and drums to our albums. Not only were we performing in some of the largest bluegrass venues in the country, we were getting great radio airplay from our singles in the southern gospel market, something very few people are able to achieve. I've always said that the sound of Jeff and Sheri is completely a gift from God in that we were brought up with much in common, yet where we differ in our musical tastes ranges from one spectrum to another. Jeff loves the country and bluegrass style, while I prefer the pop and jazz styles. When we join our voices, you begin to hear a little bit of it all.

When we began *Homefolks*, we searched for material that would lend itself to a more solid bluegrass sound, yet keeping the instruments we loved. We learned a lot about ourselves during the making of that album: always record a project that is true to you as an artist. As an artist, you are constantly creating and continuously evolving; you can never be afraid to share that part of you with others. Jeff and I have never recorded projects to please an audience or to win awards. We record projects that speak to our hearts—projects we can be proud of—and then pray that the audiences and industry peers will love what we've done.

Beyond the encouragement an award offers, it opens doors to more and better opportunities. We were asked to perform a "Jeff & Sheri" concert aboard one of the bluegrass cruises we took part in with my family. I don't think it had ever crossed our minds that we would perform as a duet away from the family until requests like this came in. Even then I could never have imagined being away from my family to perform. We traveled on a bus with Grandma and Pop, Mama, two aunts, three uncles, and two first cousins. There were ten of us onstage and twelve on the bus. Needless to say, we were close.

That's the biggest reason why our minds started wandering about the time we decided we wanted children. It was obvious there was no room for another person on the bus, let alone a baby with diapers, wipes, bottles, and a wicked schedule. Jeff and I had been married almost three years and had begun to think about the future. It was one of the most difficult choices we ever made, but when I was eight months pregnant we left the family with no dates of our own, no ideas, and no direction.

March 16, 1988—Left after school to go to Mt. Airy. Taped Earl Carney Show on the way up. I took an early pregnancy test and it turned out positive! Went to Addison's (Addison & Julianne Belangia, our oldest and dearest friends!) during lunch and held Alyssa for the first time, three days old. Substituted for Mrs. Campbell. (During the early years of our marriage, Jeff and I both worked additional jobs to supplement our income.)

March 22, 1988—Went to Dr. Echols, it's positive; I'm pregnant ☺ Six weeks pregnant, due 11/5/88.

This baby is coming into your world; you're not going into his. Make him adapt and you'll both be happier.

—Dr. J. B. Tanenbaum, my children's pediatrician

CHAPTER SIX

Heart's Desire

In November 1988, we made the first call to a promoter who had said if we ever started traveling on our own, he would be interested in booking us. We explained that we now had no job and no income with a baby due in four weeks. He told us that he would arrange a weekend in Pennsylvania if we were interested. He guaranteed a flat rate for one of the dates, but the other two would be based on a percentage of how many people attended. To be honest, we didn't know if we would draw anyone. Would twenty people come, would two hundred? We really didn't have another option, so we trusted God, loaded up our Mazda 626, and stopped by Radio Shack to purchase a $20 microphone stand on the way up.

I was very pregnant by this time, and it took us about fifteen hours to make the twelve-hour trip. We met the promoter and his family, and they graciously offered us their guest room to rest. On

Friday night we performed for his youth group's volleyball banquet, did a concert on Saturday, and sang at a church a couple of hours away on Sunday. Every audience was full, every audience bought product, and every audience embraced us. I don't remember many details about the weekend, but I remember two things: one, the promoter and his family were kind, generous, and loving; and two, they sent us home with enough money to live on for the next three weeks while we waited for the arrival of our firstborn son. Now, twenty-six years later, we still work for this promoter annually. He and his family are very dear to Jeff and me.

Madison was due November 5 according to the doctor's guess and the sonogram. The date came and went, the next week, and the next, and then Thanksgiving. I was absolutely miserable. Every weekend as Mama would leave she'd remind me not to have the baby until she got back home. She said as she left for her trip Thanksgiving weekend, "I won't ask you to wait, because I know you're miserable." Within an hour I went into labor. Twenty-six hours later, and after a forceps delivery, Madison Allen Easter was born. I had never known so much love. I had always wanted to be a mama, but I never could have imagined falling so head over heels in just one look. I wrote my first song while holding that precious baby. Talk about inspiration.

November 26, 1988 — Baby boy born at 11:47 p.m, 8 lbs., 2 oz., 21 inches long. He's beautiful, Madison Allen.

Twelve days later we sang an entire weekend of dates that Jeff had booked in Georgia and then settled in for Christmas vacation. In the meantime, we had met with and secured a booking agreement with Beckie Simmons out of Nashville. She booked our first concert December 31, 1988, and continues to book us now twenty-three years later.

Our first official date as Jeff & Sheri Easter, complete with a full band, was the Hallelujah Supper Club in Newton, North Carolina. We began working supper clubs, churches, high school auditoriums, and anywhere anyone would book us. We recorded our third project, the first on CD and our only project so far not recorded on LP vinyl. Times they were a-changin'.

Jeff and I felt very blessed to be able to travel as a family. Jeff's brother Steve ("Rabbit") joined us for our first official concert, along with longtime friend Joel Lockwood on drums. Through the years we had many configurations of the group featuring steel guitar, banjo, dobro, drums, fiddle, mandolin, electric guitar—whatever seemed to work for the time—but it was always with a band. Our families traveled with bands, and it has always been important to us to offer our audiences live music and vocals. Of all the band members who have worked with us, Greg and Charlotte Ritchie and then Rabbit have stayed the longest, working with us fourteen, twelve, and ten years respectively. We've had so much talent in this group, and we truly believe God sent every one for a season.

We purchased our first bus in 1989, a 1954 GM 4104. We bought it from my uncle Talmadge, who has owned a bus company since the 1960s. My family is frugal, and I not only learned money management in college but in the home. There's nothing like firsthand experience when it comes to running a business. Everything I did I based on my grandma's principle of "if you don't have the money, you don't get it" combined with great recommendations from an accountant and banker I trusted. We purchased the bus for $7,000 and started building the interior ourselves using plywood and two-by-fours. We refer to it now as "the rustic look"! After a while, we were able to sell the first bus and move upward into a little more comfort and a little more stability, a little at a time.

I smile as I read through my old journal entries of those early touring days:

September 8, 1988—Had publicity pictures taken for "trio" album, me, Candy Hemphill Christmas, and Tanya Goodman Sykes (Heirloom). Went by Candy's house to see the baby, Jasmine. Candy gave me a Feltman Brothers bubble suit for a boy. It's beautiful!

September 29, 1988—NQC (National Quartet Convention) Singing News Fan Awards, I presented an award with Jake Hess and sang at the Riversong Booth.

October 11, 1988 — 35 weeks pregnant according to yester-
day's sonogram. Nashville, TN to rehearse for trio album.
Ate supper with Mike and Tanya Sykes.

We always loved that the country style of our gospel music took us places outside of the gospel arena. Places like the Grand Ole Opry, vintage car shows, city and county festivals and fairs, and even to NASCAR events. A friend of ours who served as a chaplain for the Daytona 500 races invited us to sing for the chapel service for many years. Because the race was on Sundays, the drivers and crew were unable to attend church, and so they arranged a service of gospel music and speaking a couple of hours before the race. Jeff and I weren't really familiar with NASCAR, but we knew some of the more well-known drivers. During our years performing for the chapel service, we met Richard and Kyle Petty, Dale Earnhardt, Darrell and Michael Waltrip, Jeff Gordon, and many others. The Waltrips were kind enough to let us watch the races from atop their RV, and immediately we were hooked on the sport. Just like anything else in life, if you love the people, you'll love the community.

June 18, 1992 — Rustburg, VA. Seven years of marriage
and it gets better every day.

October 1, 1992 — I won Female Vocalist Alto — Singing
News Fan Awards.

In 1992, we were introduced to a man who would literally change our lives. Michael English had sung at our wedding and traveled to Nashville the next day to audition with the Bill Gaither Trio and Gaither Vocal Band. We kept in contact with Michael through the years because he was such a good friend and a huge part of our meeting in 1984. We were scheduled for a concert on Friday, and as we often do we chose to leave a little early after we heard Michael would be performing a few hours from us in Gainesville, Georgia. At the concert that evening, Michael asked Bill Gaither if we could perform a song for them. He said yes.

May 1, 1992—Gaither Vocal Band in Gainesville, GA. I sang with them (Bill Gaither, Mark Lowry, Jim Murray, and Mike English) and our group performed three songs. Bill loved it!

I don't remember a lot of details about that first performance, except that it was held in the same building where I won the talent division for the Miss Georgia Teen beauty pageant back in 1980. I also vividly remember hearing Bill Gaither behind me the entire time I sang "Roses Will Bloom Again," saying things like "Wow, what a voice! What a song! What a group! What a sound!" It was precious how verbally he showed his love for our music. After that performance, he began booking us for his concerts in Gatlinburg, Tennessee (Family Fest), and Indianapolis (Praise Gathering). In

1993, we got a phone call from Mr. Gaither inviting us to be a part of a video he would be making with many of our artist friends.

Everyone wants to know what it's like being at one of those *Gaither Homecoming* tapings. I usually tell them it's exactly what you see minus the bloopers. I'm a fan of good music. Always have been and always will be. So the videos for me were just like being allowed to witness hours and hours of good music without having to buy a ticket. In fact, for the first video we were a part of, the second in the series, I was eight months pregnant and sitting on a low ottoman without back support. I never noticed I had been there for ten hours until late into the evening. Bill and Gloria graciously offered to let us leave early, but we didn't for fear of missing something great. After we performed "Roses Will Bloom Again," Bill asked Gloria to pray for our unborn baby and us. She prayed the most beautiful prayer, and three weeks later we welcomed that precious baby girl into our lives.

Morgan Taylor Easter was born at 9:39 a.m. on September 30, 1993. Morgan literally sang melodies before she uttered a word, whereas Madison started carrying on conversations at ten months old. It is amazing how different two children raised in the same home can be.

Madison was now enrolled in kindergarten, and chicken pox was rumored to be running through the school. Being a concerned mother, I asked Madison when he got home, "Did anyone at school today have chicken pox?" To which he responded, "No, ma'am, we had rice with bologna." To this day, I'm not sure if the sentence or the combination of foods bothers me more.

With the children being five years apart, they bounced between being best friends to enemies of war their entire childhood. I used to tell people that Madison's job was not to aggravate his sister, but to destroy her. On the other hand, Madison always did like movies and creating them, and his little sister was always obliging to any role he assigned her.

October 18, 1995 — My first (detailed) journal entry since 1988, since Madison's birth. Too many changes to mention — all for the better. I'm a mother now, two times over. I'm sure I'll look at things differently now. As I am writing, I feel gentle tugs at my pants. Morgan needs attention! Something we all desire. Something a child must have to survive. God help me to keep my priorities intact. You, first in all I do, my husband and his needs, and my precious children You have blessed me with.

October 23, 1995 — 10:19 and all is quiet — sort of. The kids are at least confined to their 4x6 bed. I still hear a giggle or two every now and then, but it's peaceful.

Morgan had some hearing issues during her preschool years, which led to many of our "favorite words." Madison quickly became

Bubba, and we use that endearment to this day. At the time we had an *exkimo kiss* (eskimo spitz), we rode *excalators* (escalators) in the mall, and sometimes we listened to *wock and woll* (rock and roll). We never noticed that there was a problem. As parents, we just assumed it was a cute preschool vocabulary, but the kindergarten teacher called us in one day and recommended that she be tested.

After I scheduled the test, I noticed that I asked Morgan a question and she gently turned my face toward her and said, "I didn't hear you." She had begun to read lips to compensate for her loss of hearing. The doctor explained that sometimes petite children have drainage issues because of the smallness of their Eustachian tubes. As a singer, it devastated me that I might not have recognized something so important. After several laser and tube surgeries, she went from 82 percent hearing in one of her ears back up to 97 percent.

Morgan recorded her first CD when she was five years old, just because she loved to sing so much. She recorded another when she was nine and has sold her own CDs, purchasing them with her own money and depositing the profit into her savings account. My mama was always diligent about putting any of my money into savings, and I've done the same for my children. At the age of eleven, I set my children up with a checkbook, explained how to reconcile their accounts, and watch their income and outflow, and I've never purchased frivolous items for either of them except on special occasions like birthdays and Christmas. I think both of them appreciated the purchases more knowing how hard they had to work to get them. It has made them wiser with money management.

Morgan was easygoing and went along with almost anything we would suggest, but she wasn't always completely innocent. She relished being able to draw my attention to anything Madison did that wasn't acceptable behavior. He declares she never got caught and never allowed him to get away with anything. Typical siblings!

October 16, 1996—Another fair in Lincoln County. I believe this makes 31 years for me. Same midway, same rides, same games, same faces, that's why we go back— same faces! It's our annual "see everybody we never get to see" night. Morgan was rather comical tonight! Of course, she and "Bubba" always talk at the same time. She was asking for cotton candy, Bubba was asking for "Mama, Mama, Mama..." Morgan reached over and pinched Madison for interrupting her. By this time, I'd gotten her cotton candy and passed it to the back seat. Madison was yelling, "Morgan pinched me..." and she looked at him and said, "You can talk now"!

It reminds me of the time I was expecting Morgan. We had just played a festival up in Pennsylvania called Hinkle Fest. Some of the staff informed Madison, who was five at the time, that a Hinkle was a baby chicken. Later that week we attended a class at the hospital that explained to younger children what it would be like to welcome another child into the family. They went into detail about how wonderful it would be to have a sibling. Of course, by the time the week was over and we asked Madison what he learned, the details were a bit fuzzy. "What's a sibling, buddy?" Jeff asked. "A baby chicken," Madison exclaimed proudly.

August 13, 1998—Hot! Tired! Hoarse! Oh, do I miss my babies! We had to leave them home last night; today was the first day of school. Madison, fourth grade, and Morgan, preschool. How did that happen? I was bottle-feeding and changing diapers, and when I turned around to get a baby wipe, they were grown. I cried last night. A mother without her children isn't a mother, and I felt so worthless. I miss my mama. Monday will be nine days apart. I miss her smile! God be with us, grant us safety as we travel, and join us with those we love so deeply on Monday!

September 19, 1998—Rainsville, AL. The past week's work is showing on my face this morning. I'm tired, weak, hoarse, selfish, sleepy, and a number of other negative adjectives. The road can drain a spirit. Praise God for the rest stops along the way—a sweet smile, a sticky kiss, a hug, a word of encouragement, a good cup of coffee, and a small country church. God, please allow me to "rest" at this precious rest stop this afternoon. Allow me to receive all You have for me—I need it today. Next week is NQC (National Quartet Convention) where there will be thousands of fans, hundreds of DJs, and fellow artists, and I need to give them all something. Fill me that I may do just that. Help me be a better wife, sweeter Mama, closer friend, and wiser role model to those who need me.

February 21, 1999—I'm alone...only for a few short minutes, nevertheless I am alone. Being alone is just like being anything else; it's what you choose to make of it. Right now, being alone is a very rare and precious gift. Oh well, I'm not alone now, Morgan just "fluttered" in. She does that, you know, doesn't walk in or storm in, she flutters in, and I'm glad when she does. She makes me smile. She's five now, Madison's ten. Madison and I had a good talk a night or so ago. I feel like something's lost. Now he's accountable, responsible, and I'm not so sure I can let him be. "Roots and wings," a good parent gives roots AND wings. I'm good at the roots part, trying hard to learn the wings. God help me, and it won't be easy!

May 22, 1999—What a week! Sunday we gathered with others from our little town to watch our baby girl, "the" baby, graduate from preschool. I'll try not to close my eyes and open them to find my pen pouring out this same sentence with one exception, graduating...from high school, then college? What will be my purpose—companion, friend, wife, child, singer, but most importantly, child of God? Monday, my baby decided it was time to try her wings. She chose to have her ears pierced. I didn't want her to. She said, "That shows that I'm growing up, Mom." Richard came over at 8:30 p.m., and with much prayer, crying, arguing, ice, and nerves, we pierced them. Yes, she looks like a princess! Madison decided yesterday was his last day as a "fourth grader." It's just all happening so fast. If any Mom ever reads this, hold your babies as long as you can...

One of the greatest experiences my children were able to be a part of is the *Gaither Homecoming Kids* video series. The first video was taped when Madison was five years old up in Alexandria, Indiana, and his favorite video moment was from the *Camp Out* video where he filmed a section fishing on the creek bank with the legendary George Younce. After three videos were made, Morgan was invited to join in on the final video taped at a zoo in Indiana. Both kids made lifelong friends during the taping of those videos and cite it as one of the greatest educational as well as personal opportunities of their lifetime. It impacted Madison so greatly that he asked for a job as a camera operator on the Gaither tour from the ages of fourteen to seventeen. It was his first official paycheck.

Traveling with the Gaithers has been a wonderful experience for all of us. As I said before, I love teachers and I love to learn. Bill and Gloria are wonderful teachers who make it their life's work to impart wisdom to others. I count it a blessing for every meal I've shared with them listening to them reminisce; every trail walk filled with life lessons; every trip to foreign places where I was given pieces of history. In the absence of my daddy, God has given me some wonderful role models to shape me and carry me along this journey called life.

The Gaithers have allowed me to enjoy many trips with them, and one of my favorites was traveling to Utah in 2001 to film an episode of *Touched by an Angel*. Martha Williamson, the creator of the series, was familiar with the Gaither videos and had written a two-part episode, "Shallow Water," about a singing family called the Winslows who were dealing with healing and restoration after harsh words among the family members. It was a very touching episode about the need for forgiveness. I loved the story and I loved acting.

My children tell me I'm a "B movie" actress, and no I'm not the best at portraying another character, but I did love the experience. We met and worked with a talented bunch of writers, directors, lighting crew, and makeup artists, and an all-star cast featuring Delta Burke, David Canary, Rue McClanahan, John Schneider, Randy Travis, and John Dye. I played daughter Kay Winslow. The cast lineup for the actual singing family was in need of more females than males, so Jeff stayed home with our children. It was the longest we have ever been apart in our twenty-six-year marriage — seventy-two hours — and I was a basket case every night before bedtime.

The days were busy and full of excitement, but the nights were lonely. I remember calling home, and Morgan cried because her daddy didn't know how to make a ponytail right. I was usually the one who got up and got them ready for school each morning, so it was a new experience for them as well. Jeff was great, as usual, at making me laugh and keeping my spirits up, and truly absence makes the heart grow fonder.

Several weeks later, we gathered around the television to watch "Mama's acting debut." On the show I loaded luggage into the bay of a bus, ate in a restaurant, and sang onstage — all things I had done for years. It was an incredible experience, one I will never forget, and for the memories I am thankful.

Leaving the children at home was always hard for me, so we did everything we could to have them with us, yet not let them miss out on a good education. We always worked with the school system, staying in close contact with teachers so that the children would be able to travel. Our public school system is incredible. Most of the teachers there either taught me or graduated with me. I worked several years early in our marriage as a substitute and loved being there. I'm grateful to have had a system that understood our travels and, along with us, wanted the best education for our children. Of course, it meant extra effort for our kids to keep the grades up and make sure all deadlines were met, but so far they are grateful to have had the opportunity to do both: travel and attend public school.

We also try to make our travels educational and interesting, stopping by the Grand Canyon on our trips out West or by Niagara Falls as we headed into Canada. I remember in middle school Madison was so excited to be studying an active volcano in Hawaii that we visited. We had driven out onto the volcano and walked on its crusty surface during its dormant stage. The kids had such a grasp of geography and history just by reliving things they experienced in our travels.

Though we travel the world over to find the beautiful,

we must carry it with us or we would find it not.

—Ralph Waldo Emerson

CHAPTER SEVEN

Have Your Heart in the Right Place

W e generally travel 100,000 miles each year during our tour schedule. That's 250 million miles in this our 25th year of music and marriage. Do we feel like we have 250 million miles on our internal odometers? Some days, yes! But then again I look back and feel that the time has slipped away so quickly. So many changes, songs, friends, memories, tears, laughs, hairdos, and trends, but one thing has remained constant—the message has never changed: "Be encouraged, be blessed, trust God, have faith, praise Jesus, hold on, life may be difficult sometimes, but God is still in control." That to me is the most beautiful thing about a life dedicated to Christ—the unmovable, unshakable, steadfast love of God. (Adapted from my liner notes, *Miles and Milestones*, 2005, and for our 25th celebration in 2010)

Because of our tour schedule, I have been blessed to see many beautiful sites, to wake up to many sunrises in foreign places, to walk many pathways in faraway lands. There have been many miles and many milestones along the way. Here is a glimpse into some of my favorites.

As a child, I had the opportunity to visit Canada, Mexico, and the Bahamas fairly frequently. I traveled throughout the continental United States on trips with my family, and some of the most memorable were made so because of the people I met—the colorful characters along the way. I remember well playing in the creek in Lavonia, Georgia, behind the stage while Mama sang. I remember thinking I had never been so hot as on those summer trips to Cement, Oklahoma, or Glen Rose, Texas. I remember the love bugs in South Georgia, the sand on the beaches of Myrtle Beach, South Carolina; Virginia Beach, Virginia; and Fort Walton Beach, Florida. And one of my personal favorites was the Spanish moss dripping from the trees on Jekyll Island, Georgia. I remember the beautiful simplicity of horse and buggy rides that I witnessed on many trips to the Amish Mennonite community of Lancaster, Pennsylvania. I remember the curvy, winding roads up the mountains of North Carolina, Virginia, and West Virginia.

My life has been sprinkled with some of the most interesting places, and almost always, if a famous landmark was nearby, we made the time to see it, just because. I have pictures taken in front of Elvis' birthplace in Tupelo, Mississippi, and later in front of

Graceland. I'm smiling with several group members in front of Niagara Falls and overlooking the Grand Canyon. We've performed at Carnegie Hall, the Sydney Opera House, and the Smithsonian Institute. Recently, we had an evening to enjoy Santa Monica Pier in Santa Monica, California. I have a picture of me and my kids in front of Fred Flintstone at one of the few stops along the barren strip of Route 66 headed to the West Coast. I've been to Possum Trot, Kentucky, and Stinking Creek, Tennessee—I am not making this up!

Invariably, every trip near a theme park also prompted a visit: Six Flags Over Georgia in Atlanta; Carowinds in Charlotte, North Carolina; Kings Island in Mason, Ohio; Silver Dollar City in Branson, Missouri; Dollywood in Pigeon Forge, Tennessee; Tweetsie Railroad in Blowing Rock, North Carolina; Disneyland in Anaheim, California; and Disney World in Orlando, Florida. I've cruised to the Bahamas, Mexico, New England to Canada, and Alaska. I've seen the blue waters of the Caribbean, watched the ice calf in Glacier Bay, Alaska, and eaten some of the best seafood that still makes my mouth water in memory.

One of my favorite travel memories was the year we visited Hawaii and took our longtime friends Rickey and Karen Peck Gooch and their children, Matthew and Kari. Jeff and I had a former baby-sitter, Joyce, who was working for a travel agency and told us about a wonderful bargain on flights to Hawaii. The flights were so cheap we were able to take all eight of us. We stayed on Waikiki Beach and saw a week's worth of sightseeing in a matter of days. During the days we visited pineapple plants, walked out onto a volcano, and drove out to Pearl Harbor. At night we attended a luau and went to see Hawaiian legend Don Ho. As we were entering the building, we met Don, who made it a point to greet all of his guests. He asked if we were singers, and Karen gushed as she said, "Yes, we sing gospel music." She was so in awe of him and talked of nothing else the entire trip.

During the concert, Don called for his "gospel singing friends from Georgia" to come onstage to join him. Jeff was taking Morgan, who was three at the time, to the restroom, so Karen and I went up and began to sing. When Jeff returned, Karen motioned for him to join us. We were in the middle of singing "Amazing Grace" when Karen oozed out the sentence, "I can't believe I'm onstage with Don Ho." To this day, if anyone in our family or hers repeats that sentence, we get hysterical!

June 6 & 7, 1997—God is absolutely everywhere in nature. We're spending two days here in Kinzers, PA, with Chet and Anna Mary Stolzfus, and we're having a wonderful time being outdoors, playing by the pond, boating, fishing, and sitting! Karen Peck Gooch and all her group are here. Karen and I do a lot of sitting and sharing. Thank You God for such a dear friend I can talk to. She really understands because she knows! We've shared similar lives, and I thank

God for her to unload on! My kids love the outdoors. Jeff is fishing, and so is Rabbit (Jeff's brother, Steve). Greg and Charlotte are sitting, and we've all had restoration. Thank You God for the rest areas as we travel through this life— the areas of comfort, peace, and serenity, the areas that once again cause us to prioritize, revive, and get ready to work again!

June 20, 1997—Today I had my first speaking engage-ment, a ladies' conference in Harrisonburg, VA, and all went well. God was there, tears were there, and I felt wel-come. Jeff was by my side, pushing "play" when I sang. He's truly the "wind beneath my wings." Thank You God for the opportunity to tell others of Your faithfulness.

August 22, 1997—Quiet serenity! A rare and precious gift! I write this just after coming in from a few moments of quiet serenity. Sitting on a wooden swing carved in delicate rosebuds in the chilly, early fall air, I can hear only the birds chirping, the crickets, the soft low moan of our bus generator (which by the way is working again, PTL), and the children laughing and playing on the gym swings. John is watching them, Charlotte is watching the table, Greg is watching the concert, and I'm sure Jeff and Rabbit are watching each other. I'm watching no one, nothing, just quiet serenity. It's amazing how ten minutes in this scenery can wipe out weeks of stress. Praise God for quiet serenity. God, thank You for my family, friends, and co-workers. I am truly blessed. P.S. Cute "Morgan moment"—we were talking a couple of days ago and I mentioned she needed to brush her teeth. She replied, "Not at the dentist's, I don't think so, José!"

September 13, 1997—I love the way God has allowed me to travel. Last week we were in Hawaii. Last night in Louisville, KY, and this morning I woke up while the bus was still rolling and I realized where I was by the signs I saw. We passed a "Red Rock Peanut" truck and just beyond that a tree filled with Spanish moss, lots of flat land, and I knew I was in Georgia. Sure enough, down the road was a motel billboard, "Deep South Motel." I was right; I could tell where I was from the signs. I wish it were that easy with life. If I could see a wedding band, I could see a happily married couple. If I could see a child, I could see a smile (children aren't supposed to be sad). If I could see a Bible under someone's arm, I could see he was a Christian. It doesn't work that way. Life is uncertain, offers no guarantees. No signs. Help me, Lord, to stand firm with You through all of life's uncertainties.

March 13, 1998—Spring brings about a newness that can't be described. It is not that you are unhappy with where you've been; it's simply an excitement about where you're going!

In January 2000, we made our first trip to Europe with Bill and Gloria Gaither. Bill and Gloria had been instrumental in introducing us to so many of their fans and friends through the video recordings and concerts from as far back as 1992 in the States and Canada, and we were eager to visit Europe when Bill called and invited us to be a part of the videos there. Our first visit was to Belfast, Ireland, and yes, it's true, as Jeff was getting off the plane the pilot said "Cheerio," to which Jeff replied, "Cornflakes...Fruit Loops." You just can't make up that kind of stuff.

We had a few beautiful days searching through castles and wandering the hillsides. In one of the castles, I purchased a tiny charm engraved with "October 1945" on one side and "Forever and a Day" on the other. That charm inspired the title song from our *Forever and a Day* CD, 2003.

Later that week, we traveled to London, England, one of my top five favorite places to visit. I fell in love with all the history there— Westminster Abbey, Buckingham Palace, St. Paul's Cathedral, the Tower of London, Scotland Yard, and so many other sites that are within a few kilometers of each other. I loved it so much that I encouraged Madison and Shannon to spend a few days of their honeymoon there in 2010.

After we left London, Jeff and I, along with our friends Greg and Charlotte Ritchie, decided to spend an extra couple of days in Paris, France, while we were already in Europe. The city has such an exciting feel, and yes there is romance in the air. We visited the Eiffel Tower, shopped on the Champs Elysees, walked along the Seine, and stayed the night at a hotel with a view of the Arc de Triomphe.

February 23, 1997 — It's wonderful to fall in love! Once again, for the thousandth time, I fell in love with my husband. I woke up smiling at him while he slept. I watched him "play" all day and smiled when he acted so childishly, so excited when he'd catch "the big one" (his fishing game, of course). I watched him on stage; he looked so handsome, said all the right, funny lines, made everyone feel comfortable (that's his gift), and sang beautifully. Afterwards, on the trip home, I held him, kissed him as though I couldn't kiss him enough, told him I loved him with tears streaming down my face, and now at midnight I'm up while everyone else is asleep, writing about this wonderful mate God has blessed me with. Remembering how sweet he was in Springdale, AR, in 1984, when he walked up and said, "Hi,

Polly, remember me?" God truly gives us the desires of our heart. I love you, Jeff!

Our next trip out of the country with Bill was to Sydney, Australia. My little brother called me immediately and requested a "sidekick" pass, which in essence meant he wanted to go, and I wanted him to so badly that I paid for his flight! He has worked long hours for many years as a police officer and later as a security guard and never had the time to travel like I did. It was a treat for me to have him with me. We visited the zoo, ate in tiny coffee shops around the city, and performed at the Sydney Opera House, known for its unique architectural design. What a beautiful visit! It taught me a lot about taking time to enjoy your surroundings, though I'm not sure how much I've retained...I do try!

In 2004, we traveled to Israel with the Gaithers. Here are a few entries about the trip from my journal:

August 24, 2004 — Yesterday we left home at 3:30 a.m. for a flight out of Atlanta to JFK in New York. When we arrived, we learned that our connecting flight had been delayed three hours. Finally we boarded, but before we could take off there was another delay — engine check. We departed from JFK airport at 7:30 p.m. for our destination — Jerusalem. As we left, we were given several statistics — 5,672 miles from New York across the Atlantic. We read and chatted about three hours then dozed an hour or so. One of my favorite memories of this flight was Jeff snoring so loudly that he woke himself up. Yes, of course all of his friends and family were laughing…that's what we're here for! When I woke up we were flying over Rome, Italy, (I remember telling Jeff that's where I wanted to spend my 20th wedding anniversary next year!), then Athens, Greece, and finally, Israel. One of the interesting tidbits we learned while we were there is that there are more journalists in Jerusalem than any other part of the world, thus the reason for its constant source of news for us. Israel is about the size in area of New Jersey, and our hotel, Regency Jerusalem, is set 2,264 feet above sea level. Jerusalem is truly a "city set on a hill." Rehearsal and taping will be at David's Citadel, The Tower of David, which is also the area with ruins from Herod's palace, the place where Jesus was judged. It's midnight now and a kosher pizza is on the way!

August 25, 2004—I'm sitting here within steps of the Garden Tomb and Calvary. My heart is overwhelmed and my emotions are a wreck. Calvary, Golgotha, the place of the skull, is set on a hill for all to see. Between the short distance of the weeping at Calvary and the rejoicing at an empty tomb, I sit here realizing the difference a day makes. My favorite funny moment of today, Woody Wright described his experience of the Garden Tomb by saying, "I walked in and felt a holy hush. Then a still small voice said, 'Reggie, get over here' as only Ladye Love can" (Homecoming friends Reggie and Ladye Love Smith). As I entered Jerusalem and saw "The Great City of God" I cried, and as I left, I felt like I was leaving a familiar place, a homeland.

For our twentieth wedding anniversary, Jeff and I booked a trip to Italy, visiting Rome, Florence, and Venice. I paid the deposit and waited anxiously for the trip. Six months prior to departure, I discovered I was pregnant. To be honest, I never realized you could get pregnant after being married for twenty years. I thought by then we knew what we were doing. Oh well, the trip came and believe me I felt as though I had been married for twenty years. I waddled from the bulbous belly that left me out of balance, while Jeff hobbled alongside me with his knee scheduled for surgery when we returned.

All things considered, it was still the most wonderful vacation we had ever taken. We rented a car and drove around Rome for several days, seeing the beautiful old buildings. It changed the way I viewed the need for restoration here in our country. We are so quick to bulldoze a building that is thirty to forty years old, while Rome celebrates buildings over two thousand years old. I came home from that trip with a passion to restore the Lewis family homeplace where my mama and most of her siblings were born.

We drove the Autostrade up to Florence and spent a couple of days there taking carriage rides and walking the streets in and out of tiny shops and restaurants. It's probably a good thing I wasn't doing the math converting miles per hour to kilometers per hour! Granted, Jeff stayed with the flow of traffic, even though the flow felt much faster than what I would have liked.

We arrived in Venice on day four of the trip, and to this day I still cite it as the most beautiful city I've ever visited. I loved being surrounded by water. We had a wonderful gondola ride through the Grand Canal, saw the Rialto Bridge, visited Saint Mark's Cathedral and the Doge's Palace, and made lots of memories celebrating this marriage God has blessed us with.

Following our anniversary trip in July, I gave birth to our precious Maura Grace in October and traveled to South Africa just before Christmas in 2005. One of my favorite memories of Johannesburg was the day of rehearsal as some of the children came out to welcome us, greeting us by saying, "Jeff and Sheri, roof up above me, roof up above me," referring to Jeff's daddy's song "Thank You Lord for Your Blessings on Me." I was so touched to hear these children reciting the lines and being so grateful for the roofs that covered their heads as they lay down each night to sleep. It was precious!

November 6, 2007 — Wow! Five years since I've visited this journal; a lot has transpired in five years. Jeff & I have celebrated 22 years of marriage now, and truthfully it gets better every day! We've had an addition to our family, a beautiful surprise who marches to the beat of her very own drum—Maura Grace! Madison will be 19 in 2 weeks, and every day he's becoming more of a man. Roots have been easier than wings! Morgan is 14 and is in the 8ᵗʰ grade. She's in love with pop stars because the real thing hasn't come along yet. How beautiful she is! She'll have to trust me; someone as beautiful, inside and out, as she is won't have to search for love—it will come!

Our good friends Jeff and Amy Templeton invited us to sail to Tortola in the British Virgin Islands with them in 2006, and Jeff and I agree it was the most relaxing vacation we have ever taken. Both of us are busybodies, we have a strong work ethic, and we run at such a fast pace it's challenging for us to just sit and chill. This trip was much needed and gorgeous to boot. Jeff owns a travel agency and is my kind of guy, offering details about the history of places as we traveled. He and Amy have been our friends for many years and even asked that Jeff and I would stand in with them for their wedding in Charleston, South Carolina, years ago. Jeff is a see-and-do type of personality, and I'm more of a listen-and-reflect—this trip offered both.

Here are some of my journal entries:

November 12, 2006—I woke up this morning to the smell of coffee. We arrived in St. Thomas, U.S. Virgin Islands, yesterday around 2 p.m. with Jeff and Amy Templeton and their friends, Dave and Christie. Rickey and Karen Gooch met us here for a 6-day voyage aboard a beautiful catamaran. We had lunch in town and then hopped aboard the 50-minute Fast Ferry to Road Town, Tortola. When we arrived, we began to unpack in our staterooms. Jeff and I are staying in the bedroom, starboard aft...before the week is over, I'll be tying nautical knots! Ken, our captain, explains that when boats would pull into the harbor to unload merchandise, they began using a system of pulling in with the left side of the boat towards the "port" and the right side facing the "stars" or starboard.

My devotions this morning are Psalm 133, "Behold, how good and how pleasant it is for brethren to dwell together in unity." Today we sailed into some of the rocky areas just outside Tortola, and everyone went snorkeling. (My idea of snorkeling was getting in the water with my mask, peeking a glimpse, and then jumping back on board, never letting go of the boat! I don't swim well and opted to read in the sunshine instead. They showed me pictures and it was lovely!) We sailed into Cooper Island around 5 p.m. and ate at an island beach restaurant. We laughed a lot!

November 13, 2006—Another beautiful day! Boats in the harbor near Cooper Island surround me, the waters are smooth, and the sunshine is already warming my shoulders. Today we're heading toward the island of Virgin Gorda. We are en route and spot a sinking ship, probably a freight carrier. Ken thinks it must have sunk sometime last night. The waters are a bit rougher today and I am reminded of the analogy that God is our sure foundation. If I keep my eyes on the "stable" surfaces around me (the islands) instead of the boats and the crashing waves, I don't feel sick or threatened. In life, we sometimes get our eyes off God and instead focus on the circumstances around us and we panic. We must, as Paul says, keep our eyes on "the prize." We arrive at The Baths of Virgin Gorda and start our 1-2 hours of exploration. It's a magnificent area of rocks that appear as though they were purposely stacked one upon another. Later, a ferry takes us to The Bitter End, a resort that can only be reached by water. We had a late lunch and sailed to Saba Rock tonight for dinner.

November 14, 2006—It's hard to believe you can have such wonderful weather day after day, but we have been blessed.

We sailed most of the day and anchored at Foxy's Harbor, one of the most well-known locations in the Virgin Islands. Foxy's is a little shack on an island with wooden tables and benches. It's an open-air restaurant known for its delicious cuisine and of course its owner, Foxy. We had a nice visit with him and made pictures. He's been here since 1968 and has now opened his second restaurant on the island. It is believed he still maintains business ownership. The restaurant has become known throughout the world. "Live da life."

Our third trip to Europe included several locations we hadn't been able to visit previously. Glasgow, Scotland, was lush with its green, softly rolling hillsides, and Siegen, Germany, was such a quaint town with wonderful old buildings. I really enjoyed our trip to the Netherlands and our visit to the Anne Frank museum. Because of the destruction of war in Rotterdam, the buildings are newer, more modern, whereas Amsterdam has the historical beauty of an Old World city and cobblestone streets. Norway was the final stop on the tour and was filled with precious people who loved our brand of gospel music.

I've been afforded the opportunity to see places that others haven't seen. I've walked pathways unfamiliar to most. I've stored so many wonderful memories of travel, and for every opportunity I am humbled and most thankful.

CHAPTER EIGHT

Absence Makes the Heart Grow Fonder

My wonderful Grandma and Pop celebrated seventy-seven years of marriage. What a legacy of love! Theirs is a story worth repeating. Grandma was fifteen and Pop twenty when they fell in love. They wanted to marry and chose to elope. Grandma's daddy had been ill and was sleeping downstairs in the family room, which prevented Grandma from leaving through the front door to meet Pop. So Pop took a nearby ladder, placed it up to her second-story bedroom window, and they slipped away to a neighboring county to wed. That's what love does; it makes you trust your heart in spite of what your head may tell you. My grandma was probably the greatest Christian influence in my life, and despite her quiet nature she was very bold about her faith. Her love for God and her dedication to her husband and children spoke volumes about the legacy of love she left behind.

One afternoon, a friend of ours helped Jeff and me pen this song in honor of that legacy of love.

She's Loved Him for So Many Years

It was a cool night in October, in a little Georgia town
He put a ladder to the window, and she came climbing down
He was just a boy of twenty, she was a girl just turned fifteen
But they slipped away into the night with nothing but their dreams

Times were hard and life was simple in 1925
But their need to be together kept their love alive
He loved this preacher's daughter and carried her away
He plowed that red dirt farmland for a dollar a day

And she's loved him for so many years
A moment never slipped by that she didn't think of him
Though many times the road was hard, faith never disappeared
She's loved him for so many years

Eight times the pain of childbirth, she thanked the Lord for
all of them
Then she felt the grief when the Lord required she give one
back to Him
She never has forgotten, she remembers to this day
For there's a little pair of overalls she's never thrown away

And she's loved him for so many years
A moment never slipped by that she didn't think of him
Though many times the road was hard, faith never disappeared
She's loved him for so many years

She has stood like an oak tree through all of this life's storms
But everyone who knows her knows where her strength
comes from
At times when she's too tired to stand, she falls down on her
knees
For her trust is in a God she knows will meet her every need

And she's loved Him for so many years
A moment never slipped by that she didn't think of Him
Though many times the road was hard, faith never disappeared
She's loved Him for so many years

Sheri Easter/Aaron Wilburn/Jeff Easter
Copyright 1994

Jeff and I recorded this song on our project *The Gift*. It was simply my way of honoring the love my grandma had for her husband, her child, and God. In later years she developed dementia, and although it was difficult, there were moments that made us smile. I wrote about this in an article in November 2002.

Do You Still Love Me?

Grandma and Pop are now 92 and 97 and both experiencing symptoms of dementia. On more than one occasion, I've been required to "introduce" myself to them, sometimes with an understanding "Oh yes, that's right" and sometimes with nothing more than a blank stare. However difficult dementia can be, it still gives us moments of humor from time to time. The other day, Pop sat down beside of Grandma, patted her leg, and asked, "Do you still love me, Ma?" After carefully searching his face, she replied, "If you're Roy Lewis, I do!"

Grandma passed away at the age of ninety-two in 2003, and Pop passed away thirteen months later at ninety-eight. When Grandma passed away, I received the call around 10 a.m. Jeff came to me with the phone and explained that it was Mama and she was very upset. Here are some of my journal entries from February 8 and 9, 2003.

February 8, 2003—I took the phone and Mama was crying hysterically and repeating over and over, "Mama died," almost as if she were convincing not only me but also the both of us. My mind searched her words for clarity. Grandma had been fine, she was strong, and Pop had been so feeble; we had all assumed, with his declining health and five-year seniority to Grandma, he would go first.

Jeff and I went to the funeral home, and they graciously allowed us to go into the room with her body. I held her hand and stroked it, feeling the smooth cold skin. I kissed her cheek, now too cold from death. I brushed the hair back from her face and touched behind her ear where there was still warmth. It was so comforting, I cherished the moments and thanked them all for letting me spend a few selfish moments with the woman who had shaped and molded my life.

I was assured that the shell of her mortal body was simply that—a shell, an empty shell, no longer housing the beautiful spirit we loved so deeply. It comforted me to see its emptiness, for I am fully assured that she is with Jesus. Heaven for her was a reality, and she now knew its splendor.

We went into the front room filled with caskets, and this time was so much more peaceful than it had been for me nineteen years ago after Daddy's death. I was fully aware of the technical part of dying and now felt more at ease with the process.

February 9, 2003—4:07 a.m. and I'm wide awake, expecting Mama to call around 8 a.m. for me to take her and Janis to the funeral home. I began to write down every detail I could remember so that I could share them with Mama and my children in years to come. Daddy's funeral/visitation time is such a fog I hardly remember any details, and that frustrates me. I got a load of clothes washing and drying and began to pack Jeff's clothes for the cruise. Up until last night, we weren't sure we'd go. But I thank God for two full days to spend with Grandma and the family, and we've decided to go ahead to Mexico.

Mama called and said we'd leave in a half hour. I drove, after Mama met me, and then we picked up Janis. We entered the funeral home through the front door, and I cautioned them that the casket was in the left front room against the left wall. I prepared them because I remembered how hard it was seeing Daddy for the first time.

At the cemetery, I noticed Moseley's tombstone was engraved "Gone but Not Forgotten" and realized for the first time in almost 70 years, Grandma is having the opportunity to hold, kiss, and rock her baby boy of 4 years old who preceded her in death. Heaven is real.

After leaving the cemetery, I stopped by to get Jeff and the children to go to Grandma's house for lunch. The entire family had gathered, and as I was leaving, I hugged and kissed Pop and told him I had to go. He asked while I was still hugging him goodbye, "Where's Pauline?" I could hear sniffles and groans behind me as family members were startled at his question.

"Pauline died, Pop," I said, with tears streaming down my face.

"No, MY Pauline," he stated with clarity.

"She died, Pop." He began to cry.

"Oh, no, why didn't somebody tell me?"

"We tried, Pop, but your medicine makes you confused and you just forgot. "

"She never caused me any trouble."

"No, Pop, she never caused any of us trouble."

"When did she die?"

"Yesterday morning, remember you said you missed her at breakfast?"

"Did she suffer?"

"No, Pop, she just went to sleep and never woke up, just like my daddy."

"Yeah, Elzie died like that."

"You remember that, Pop?"

"Yeah, he was young."

"Yes, he was only 50; you've already been blessed to live almost double that."

After an hour of questions, answers, crying and wiping his tears, hugging and kissing, Jeff and I and our children left to go home. Pop had finally comprehended the devastating news.

They wheeled Pop in the funeral home, and I was waiting at the casket for him. He cried, said he recognized her, that she was pretty, and said again, "She never caused me any trouble; she was kind and never liked confusion."

I asked if he'd like to hold her hand. He did, so I lifted his hand to hers and he said, "Oh, it's so cold. Mom's hands were always so warm and smooth."

Little Roy asked if he wanted to sing to her, starting Pop off on "Let Me Call You Sweetheart." All of us kids, grand-kids, and great-grands wept. He sang one line of "Come Sit by My Side, Little Darlin'" and then said he didn't feel like singing anymore.

I stayed until everyone went home, and when it was just me and Grandma, I tucked the folds in her jacket, straightened her jewelry, held her hand, kissed her cheek, and whispered that I loved her, I missed her, and was so proud of how pretty she looked (everyone said she looked like Polly). I told her she had so many friends there. I told her to hug Daddy for me, and I left the funeral home.

The way someone handles death is such a personal experience. Because of having to face death so early in my life, I always try to encourage people to grieve however they need to grieve. It is a process. It is a part of life.

Thirteen months after we said goodbye to Grandma, Pop took his last breath in the hospital with his youngest son by his side. Little Roy and Pop had worked side by side for many years, and it seemed fitting that they were together for Pop's final moments. "I love you's" had always been understood yet not spoken between Little Roy and Pop. While they were alone, Little Roy told him, "I love you, Pop," and he breathed his final breath.

CHAPTER NINE

Home Is Where the Heart Is

Jeff and I are both pretty practical when it comes to everyday choices in living life. We believe the Scripture that says if a man doesn't work, he doesn't eat, and we've never been afraid of work. Both of us have held jobs, sometimes multiple jobs, since we were fifteen years old. Everything we have accomplished is because we weren't afraid to try. I'm a planner. I do much better when I have a detailed schedule. Jeff flies by the seat of his pants all day, every day!

Early in our marriage he looked at me one Tuesday morning and said he wanted to go see his family. I said "Sure" and pulled out the date list. He then went on to explain that he meant "right now," a term completely unfamiliar to me. After a couple of moments of trying to rationalize such a ridiculous idea, I realized there was no need for rationalization—this was doable! I grabbed my toiletries bag and a change of clothing, and we left for the five-hour trip to Mt. Airy! That trip was the first of many impromptu visits over the years. Because of his children, Jeff and I were always making unplanned trips about every six weeks to visit.

Our entire marriage has been that way. Jeff's always ready to move at a moment's notice, and I need time to study and prepare. The beautiful thing about the combination is that we do need to wait sometimes, and we need to be flexible enough to move at others. Together we really do find the best in life! In spring of 1990, Jeff and I were young parents to Madison and living in a singlewide mobile home. I had drawn up house plans and collected everything I ever wanted in a home for the previous five years of our marriage, hoping one day to build. With our disposable income at the time, we had even purchased tubs, toilets, and porch railings from salvage yards of overstocked or discontinued items. We stored them in our shed and waited for the right time to build.

The shed is a story of its own. Jeff and I are known for our "projects." It's not unusual for friends to visit and for us to have just knocked out a wall in the foyer in order to expand a room. A friend of ours had an old building in his backyard, and because it was weathered he wanted it removed. For two weeks Jeff and I and a few friends made trip after trip taking the building down board by board and rebuilding it on our land behind our mobile home. The building was free, and after a few years, some siding, new windows, doors, and a roof, we had built our recording studio in our backyard for an almost apologetically low price!

So for about three years Jeff and I collected items for our dream home, including light switch covers and faucets, windows and doors, storing them in our shed. The house plans had been drawn and most of the items purchased. I remember once we were walking through Lowe's and saw a beautiful light fixture marked down to $20. For years that fixture hung in our foyer entrance. Jeff and I both like bargain hunting, and it's a pastime that really pays off! My goal for building our home was to build *the* home for our lifetime. I grew up in one house my entire young life, I visited one grandparents' home, and I wanted that stability for my children, so it was important to think of the big picture when the home was designed. I wanted a house that we could live in with all the amenities of a restful place of retreat. We typically travel three days each week and return home for four, so I wanted to enjoy our time at home.

In May 1990, with some good friends' help, we pulled the strings for our house-to-be, and late one night went outside, standing where the front door would be, and held hands and prayed. We asked that God would lead us, that He would provide, and that He would give us the knowledge and strength to build our home. Early the next morning the first bulldozers arrived to clear the land.

Jeff and I were blessed with friends who offered to build, yet allowed us to work alongside them. We had an electrician who donated his time and some materials and allowed us to do the wiring with his supervision. We had a plumber who taught Jeff how to plumb the first bathroom, and we finished the others. We installed our air conditioning/heat system with several of Jeff's family members. We installed our hardwood floors, borrowing the tools from friends in the carpentry business, and I painted. Notice all the other jobs began with "we" and painting began with "I." Jeff doesn't like to paint!

We labored for six months and moved into our home in September 1990. It is the same home we live in today, twenty-one years later. It is the home that all of our children remember as their childhood home. There are porches for resting, a game room for playing, a pool for outdoor fun, quiet rooms for reading, and an office for working.

Having an office in the home has allowed me to be a mama to my children, and having a studio in the backyard has afforded Jeff the privilege of being an at-home daddy. For ten years Jeff opened up the studio to the public and did many recordings, but as our travel schedule increased, our free time for studio decreased and we closed the studio to the public. We still do all of our vocal recordings here and it makes it so much easier than before we built. For our first four or five projects, we had to drive six hours to Nashville, staying for a week for tracks, then return home another six hours, knowing there would be two more stints like that in the near future to record vocals and then mix the project. Our studio has given us many hours at home that we would have sacrificed without it. Madison loves spending time there working on demos and rehearsing. All three of

Morgan's projects were recorded there, and eighteen of our twenty-six projects have had some of or the entire project recorded in our backyard.

October 26, 1995—Slept in! 11:30 came and I thought I'd be rested. Seems the opposite is true. I don't seem to get nearly as much done on days like this. About 5:15 I got a shower and started getting ready for my date. Jeff is taking me out for my birthday. We took the '49 Ford on Jeff's insistence. We stopped for gas and the entire truck cab was filled with smoke—"a wire touched" was all Jeff said. Here I am all dressed up jumping out of this "bad" looking truck (that's cool for those of another generation). Jeff pulled out a roll of black tape and we were back on the road in ten minutes. He's good at that. We ate at Soap Creek Restaurant near the house, crab legs, baked potato, and salad. Headed for home, just the two of us; it's nice to get reacquainted every now and then. Lord, I love this man you have blessed me with!

October 28, 1995—"And they're off" is truly how I've felt today. Hurry, hurry! We met Karen Peck and New River at Crowne Plaza in Houston and later went together to the Houston Galleria mall. We had a blast. We all met for Mexican at 1 p.m. then left for the concert at 3 p.m.

I almost bought an outfit but talked myself out of it, only later to regret leaving it behind. To my surprise, Jeff borrowed someone's keys, carried me back to the mall, and bought the outfit. He goes above and beyond the call of duty as a husband. I'm truly blessed. The concert was a lengthy one, and afterwards we were all exhausted with a twelve-hour trip ahead of us. Lord, give us strength!

November 1, 1995—Cleaned all day again! A woman's work really is never done. Jeff and I put up a decorative shelf along Morgan's bedroom wall to hold her Barbies. It's really nice. It was an all-day project, but we had fun doing it together. Projects like that keep us friends!

October 8, 1996—As a child, I never understood why adults always talked about "My, how time has flown!" To me, it seemed to drag mercilessly. Would school EVER get out? Would Friday nights EVER arrive? Today, I look at my last journal entry as if it were a week ago, not a year! My, how time has flown! So much has happened, but I've been too busy to jot it down. It's really sad to be too busy for oneself. So these fifteen minutes are mine. Madison is at school (second grade, honor roll, I have to brag!). Jeff is probably on his way home from taking Madison (to school)—that's our deal. I'm up at 7:30, dress and feed Madison, then

Daddy's shift starts at 7:50, the drive. Morgan is watching TV (Doug, I think) in her room, and I'm enjoying "me." Being alone is a priceless treasure. Being lonely is a devastating end. Thank You God for allowing me to be alone instead of lonely. Praise the Lord for His eternal presence in our lives!

As my children approached their teenage years, I decided it would be a good time for me to go back to school to get my master's degree in business. It was obvious that the landscape of business had changed drastically since my college years, and with my children being older and not needing so much of my time, it seemed like the perfect plan. I enrolled in Brenau Online College in 2003 and began my studies. I've always loved school and I'm a good student, so it was quite natural for me to want to get my MBA. For two years I studied every day of the week and turned in my work on the weekends while I traveled. I loved being back in school, and I'm grateful that my family sacrificed many hours to allow me that opportunity.

Our music, marriage, and family have all been so intertwined that it's hard to see where one area starts and another ends. When I think of family vacations, it usually begins after a long concert tour, a concert on a cruise, or a particular awards program. When Jeff and I married, we chose a Tuesday for the date so that it wouldn't interfere with the concert schedule, and our babies were planned for the fall because it's the time of year that our dates slow down a bit. Well, all but one of our children was planned!

Don't you just love a surprise? In 2002, just before my thirty-ninth birthday, I began having difficulties with my voice. As a singer I have to pace myself, knowing my body well enough to know when to rest. A singer who doesn't rest doesn't have a voice to sing. We had just completed two weeks of cruises, filled with thousands of people to talk to, hours of concerts to sing, and a schedule that allowed very little time to rest. By the end of the second cruise, my voice was gone. I tried resting over the next couple of weeks, but it never seemed to be enough. I was afraid and knew that I needed to see a specialist. I made an appointment with Vanderbilt Voice Clinic and discovered I had developed two small nodules. They immediately placed me on complete voice rest and gave me an extended dosage of steroids. For a singer, complete voice rest means no concerts. My calendar was full.

We decided to hire someone to take my place onstage while I was on voice rest, and I would continue to travel to all of the dates to meet the people and sign autographs. For someone who loves to talk as much as I do, complete vocal rest is ultimate frustration! I wore a button announcing to the world that I couldn't speak, I carried a dry-erase board with me at all times, and I became very good at sign language within my circle of family and close friends. There was only one problem with the system: Jeff doesn't spell well, and he knows no sign language. There were times that I could sign the first letter of what I was about to say, and Charlotte or the kids knew exactly what I meant, while there were other times I would spell an entire sentence or sign several words and Jeff was still clueless. One of my favorite stories was when Jeff was deciding which route to take for one of our trips. I was trying to give him my opinion and began to sign the route through a nearby town. I signed M, C, C, O, R, in an attempt to spell McCormick, and Jeff screamed out "Roscoe," referring to our bus driver at the time!

For anyone who has ever been on steroids, you know that weight gain is one of the side effects. I gained ten pounds within a week and another twenty over the course of the next year. I became so frustrated that I went to an endocrinologist because I was dieting and still continuing to gain weight. The morning of my appointment to get my results, I visited my gynecologist, who informed me that at forty-one I was pregnant. I had taken an at-home pregnancy test that morning at 5:30 a.m. Jeff says that's the best place to take one of those! I cried when I saw the results. I woke Jeff up saying, "It's got two lines. It's got two lines!" He reached for his bifocals on the nightstand to view the results and exclaimed, "If you have to get your bifocals to read a pregnancy stick, you might be too old to have a baby!"

Jeff and I were about to celebrate our twentieth wedding anniversary and had a seventeen-year-old and a twelve-year-old who had been planned almost to the day when all of a sudden, as Gomer Pyle would say, "Surprise, surprise, surprise!" My first call was to apologize to Madison, who I thought would be furious. He didn't answer. My second call was to my mama, who heard my voice and asked why I was upset. I explained, "Mama, I'm pregnant and I'm old." She laughed. My third call was to Morgan, who jubilantly announced it to her gymnastics class. We finally got a call through to Madison, who said, "How could I be angry? This is great!" I was so relieved. Then Jeff's phone rang and it was Mark Lowry. We told Mark and within twenty minutes it was on the Internet. I always make sure Mark knows everything important I want others to know; he's my voice to the outside world!

Maura has been a gift to our entire family. With her spunk and wit, she makes life fun for all of us. She truly has been the best of surprises. At the age of forty-two, I had just completed my graduate studies for my MBA in business leadership, I had given birth to baby number three, and my precious Mama had been diagnosed a couple years prior with Parkinson's disease. My plate seemed awfully full, and I couldn't imagine how I could take on any more challenges at this point in my life.

God whispers to us in our pleasures, speaks in our
conscience, but shouts in our pains: it is His
megaphone to rouse a deaf world.

—C.S. Lewis

My family, The Lewis Family,
in the mid-1950s, while they were
recording WJBF Channel 6 in
Augusta, Georgia

Me, in my bedroom,
about age three

Singing into my jump rope
microphone on the hearth
in our den

Homecoming Queen
1979-1980
Photo credit: Garnett Wallace

The last family photo we
made before Daddy's death in 1984
Photo credit: Stan Wilkinson

June 18, 1985
Photo credit:
Stan Wilkinson

With Jeff's daughter, Misty, and his son, Josh

Jeff and me with The Lewis Family Photo credit: Stan Wilkinson

One of the early configurations of our group, with drummer Jarrett Dougherty and Jeff's brother Steve "Rabbit" Easter

With two beautiful music legends, Dottie Rambo and Connie Smith

Our family with the Gooches and Don Ho in Hawaii

With Gloria Gaither

With Bill Gaither

With Vestal Goodman

With Jake Hess

With the love of my life

On the set of *Touched by an Angel*

With Rue McClanahan and Delta Burke

With my sweet Mama

With Grandma

With Pop

With Charlotte Ritchie

Singing with Mama

With Jeff in Alaska

In 2007, Photo credit:
Kim Lancaster

Madison in Alaska

Morgan in 2009, Photo credit:
Russ Harrington

Maura in 2007
Photo credit: Kim Lancaster

We Are Family with The Lewis Family,
The Easter Brothers, and us,
Photo credit: Mercer Harris

Our family in Alaska

My first publicity photo after breast cancer
Photo credit: Russ Harrington

With Dolly Parton
Photo credit: Aaron Crisler

With my firstborn
on his wedding day

The Easters
Photo credit: Andy Donnan

With my brother, Scott, and his family
Photo credit: Andy Donnan

Our group today
with drummer Kyle Calloway
Photo credit: Paul Wharton

At the Nashville Grammy party with
Connie Smith, Marty Stuart, and
Ricky Skaggs, Photo credit:
Aaron Crisler

At the Grammy party with
Lady Antebellum
Photo credit: Aaron Crisler

With Karlene and George Beverly
Shea and Julie Andrews
Photo credit: Aaron Crisler

With Andy Andrews
Photo credit: Aaron Crisler

With Little Jimmy Dickens at
The Grand Ole Opry
Photo credit: Aaron Crisler

CHAPTER TEN

Heartache

My job in the public's eye requires a balancing act of personal and private lives. I have always believed that I should share as much as I was comfortable with, with those who invest in my life. I've shared details about my children, my marriage, and my faith throughout the years of my travels. It's sometimes hard to share the more personal parts because you open yourself up to a very vulnerable place, yet when I see an opportunity to encourage others because of my pain, I try to be very honest and speak from my heart. In mid-2008, I made the decision to begin a series of blogs in order to offer encouragement through my pain.

July 3, 2008—I watched the sun rise this morning! It's one of my favorite ways to celebrate life—I usually do it on vacations or just after a battle...times that I can truly appreciate it. Yesterday at 4 p.m., I received a call from my newly acquired surgeon informing me that I had breast cancer. I have breast cancer. I feel almost as if I should type it 100 times to remind me not to do it again, just like in grammar school—I will not talk in class (that was always my sentence of choice!). I cried until it hurt and then I cried more. Morgan was sitting with me when I got the call. Jeff, Madison, and everyone on our bus quickly came to the front lounge and along with me were broken. I wanted to say "I'm sorry" but I stopped myself because I knew they'd remind me that it wasn't my fault. Jeff called my mama, my brother, and several of my closest friends because I couldn't speak.

I found the lump last October, scheduled a mammogram, received the news that it was normal, and lived with a false security until last week when an online nosedive into the percentage of reliability of mammograms sent me rushing to schedule another checkup. The nurse asked if I had a surgeon, and I waited for the appointment. Wednesday, I drove down only to find out that he had been called in on an emergency surgery and I would have to reschedule the appointment for Monday.

On Thursday morning I woke up praying, "God, You're going to have to get me through this weekend. I can't do it on my own." I opened my Bible to a random page, and the first words I read were in a passage from Mark 5: "Don't be afraid. Just believe." I shared that all weekend, not specifying my need, but simply to remind myself and my audience that God IS faithful. Monday morning the surgeon examined me by sonogram and asked if I minded if he did a biopsy because it didn't look normal. I wanted a cyst. I wanted it aspirated. I didn't want a biopsy, and I certainly didn't want to wait another 48 hours for test results. Nevertheless, I waited until yesterday and then again heard things I didn't want to hear like breast cancer, mastectomy, and lumpectomy/radiation. We had previously gotten a call from Charlotte that Greg's daddy, Jerry Ritchie, had passed away after a long battle with cancer. Jeff briefly worked with Jerry in the early '80s, and we of course loved him because he was Greg's dad. We had planned to be at the funeral today...

I wonder how many times in my life I've used the word "planned"? My schedule doesn't have an opening for cancer. I'm a scheduler and a very good one at that, but even I can't schedule life onto a calendar.

I'm leaving in an hour to meet with my surgeon and discuss my course of action. Please pray that we make wise decisions. I may not be able to schedule life, but I am assured that God can.

Writing my blogs helped me communicate to my audiences exactly where I was in my journey, but my private journal entries were much more candid and expressed the deeper pain I was feeling.

June 30, 2008—I went in today for what I had hoped to be a cyst. My heart wanted only an aspiration procedure and

then I'd be free of this lump that has plagued my body and my mind for the past eight months. My doctor asked if we could do a sonogram. Soon after he began, he said that it didn't "look normal" to him, and would I mind having a biopsy. I quickly agreed but all the while my heart was sinking. They told me I could dress, and when I went into the private dressing area, I cried.

July 2, 2008—[After the news] Madison wondered how I'd be able to sing in a couple of hours. I reassured him by saying, "Because I believe those songs before I get on stage."

July 3, 2008—After much prayer and many tears, Jeff and I agreed a mastectomy would be best, and hopefully I could live cancer-free. We were sent for an MRI to be certain the other breast was healthy. While waiting for the MRI, Jeff drove me to Riverwalk and we walked along the water's edge in disbelief of the mountain we were facing. The MRI was such a scary experience, and I was so glad to get home after five hours of doctors, offices, and hospitals. I don't do sick very well.

Breast cancer is something I faced in life, a journey I endured...it does not define me. It is not who I am.

—Sheri Easter

July 8, 2008—Surgery today. Went in for prep at 8:45 a.m. I don't remember anything until I was placed in my room afterwards. It was so great seeing my kids—Melissa brought them by.

July 9, 2008—Jeff slept at the hospital with me, and I'm sure he didn't rest. I'm told I should be released today. I get to go home. Jeff has to leave for Indiana tonight. I insisted; folks are counting on him being there! Julianne brought supper.

July 10, 2008—Lots of tightness, swelling, and pain. Jeff, Morgan, and Shannon sang tonight—audience understood. Grace brought supper. Madison is staying home with me.

July 11, 2008—I've received so many beautiful flowers and goody baskets. Scott and the boys came by. Melissa and Melynda have been watching Maura or me while Madison took the other responsibility. Julianne's bringing supper again. The pain is pretty rough, but I'm getting better using Tylenol instead of pain meds. My chest looks horrible, but I'm trying to remember it will get better. We found out yesterday that my doctor removed 20 lymph nodes and only two had cancer, so I am facing chemotherapy. Will know more Tuesday and Thursday at doctors' appointments.

July 14, 2008 — Jeff's home. It's so much better when he's here. I sure missed him and Morgan. I'm hoping they will remove the drainage tubes tomorrow. They really reduce my mobility.

July 15, 2008 — My first day out of the house. My doctor said everything looked good and he removed the drainage tubes — very painful! Slept most of the remainder of today. Removed bandages — it looks awful!

July 16, 2008 — Rested. Watched movies and TV with Jeff. Pain is still pretty bad. No one should be as blessed as I have been — but it's just so hard to accept the unfairness of cancer.

Again and again, I turned to writing to get my feelings out, such as the blog entries below:

July 17, 2008 — I've been quiet lately. I find that I hear much better when I'm not talking. Now more than ever I simply want to hear God's voice. There have been many decisions for which I needed direction and many voices speaking encouragement, and

I've enjoyed listening…. In hindsight, I am certain we made the right choice. I am healing well and have received so many, many phone calls, emails, and cards—may God bless each of you for your deep concern and prayers you are offering. I am physically healing as the doctors expected and emotionally fragile as you can well assume. I had a "crash and burn" moment just last night. All the "what ifs," "why me's," and "it's just not fair's" made me fall into Jeff's arms, and he held me while I cried. This morning I am grateful for a caring husband and incredibly understanding children, in addition to encouraging news from my oncologist. We are in a state of grace when I report that we have chosen to have chemotherapy as a preventive measure, in doing all that we can to become 100% cancer free. My treatments will begin in the latter part of August and continue through mid-December. Please continue to pray for our family as we walk through this journey into healing. According to the oncologist, I should have more than one reason to celebrate this Christmas!

July 17, 2008—We met with my oncologist—good news, a mastectomy alone saves 82 of 100 women, chemo increases that number to 91, Tamoxifen for 5 years increases it to 93%. I'm going for 100% cancer free! We scheduled an echogram, bone scan, CT scan, Pet scan, and a surgery to put a port in place. As I was leaving, we saw a friend of ours who has been battling cancer a while now. My

heart broke for him and his wife—now I know how to be thankful again!

July 18, 2008—I'm in Winchester, KY. I decided to travel and sing this weekend. I slept in Morgan's bunk to protect myself. I'm starting to "feel" the tissue expander now that the surgical area is waking up. It's really uncomfortable. Yesterday the oncologist mentioned explaining the hair loss to Maura—she's only two! Wow, how do you do that? I sang tonight, but I'm sore.

July 19, 2008—Jackson, TN, with Karen Peck. She came over and visited this morning. Morgan ordered me a book after googling "explaining to a toddler cancer and hair loss." I hope it helps. We ate at Casey Jones with precious Dr. Rhear and his wife, Judy. It was he who Jeff called when I had my "crash and burn" a few days ago. I walked onstage tonight wearing about the only outfit I could that wouldn't show my loss. The audience stood and welcomed Morgan and me as we made our way to center stage with Jeff. We sang "Life Is Great & Gettin' Better" and meant it, then "Praise His Name." At the end of the song, the entire audience stood and applauded for what seemed like an eternity. I've never before witnessed such an outpouring of love. Later I sang "She Loved" and it happened again.

We sang "Thank You Lord" and Morgan began to cry. She sang "Jesus Knows Me" and more ovations occurred. As we exited, another explosion of applause and standing! I am amazed. I am loved!

July 23, 2008—Doctors' appointments today. One was a follow-up and he gave me some exercises to help regain the use of my arm. I told him it was a feeble attempt at what I really wanted to say to someone who's saved my life, but thank you. At the other appointment, I had my stitches removed and my first 100 cc's of saline solution put into my tissue expander. The tiny mound is beginning to look like a breast. Weird, there was no real pain, just pressure.

July 24, 2008—Echogram this morning to be sure my heart is strong enough for the chemo. Macon, GA, tonight for a concert.

July 25, 2008—Dahlonega, GA, with Karen Peck and all. Madison had a breaking moment. I had just told Jeff two or three days ago to talk with him and see if he was handling all of this well. He obviously wasn't. For about twenty minutes, he rolled his eyes, accused me of exaggerating the danger, and mocked. Afterward, he broke down and cried, apologized, and confessed that it's hard to believe in someone who CAN heal but doesn't. I understand his hurt. We've all had that question—finding our own answer is the difficult part. He will; he's a great kid.

July 27, 2008—Montgomery, AL—Greg K. rode with us. His wife, Beth, passed away last May, and I thought maybe I should avoid talking about my cancer; instead he talked about it the bulk of the trip. Sometimes we need to say and remember the ugly stuff so we can appreciate everything in between.

July 28, 2008—Bone scan, University Hospital—almost four hours. We're praying for no "hot spots"!

July 29, 2008—I'm up early. I walked today for the first time since before surgery (1 mile in 16 ½ minutes—not too bad!) We're taking Morgan to see the Jonas Brothers tonight.

July 30, 2008—100 cc's more of saline solution into the tissue expander at my appointment today. Within an hour, I could barely breathe and had to go back on pain meds.

August 5, 2008—Went to have my port placed today at 1 p.m. It's a little uncomfortable, but not terrible. The orig-

inal surgery area is much better. Procedure was odd in that I was given a mild nerve pill then taken to the operating table. I was then given an IV antibiotic and some anesthesia, and I remembered some of the activity but not much.

August 6, 2008—Doctor's appointment for more cc's of saline (only 30 this time, so it's not as painful as last week). Had to cancel Japanese food tonight; too much pain.

August 10, 2008—Worked all day with office and laundry! Today is the first day I've felt like myself in over a month. I really feel good!

August 11, 2008—Great news today—all tests, bone scans, CT scans, and echocardiograms came back clear, no tumors, no metastasizing. Praise God!

August 12, 2008—Six-week follow-up. Preparing for Alaskan Cruise.

August 25, 2008—I figured I might as well go ahead and journal my thoughts today as it is a monumental day! My first day of chemotherapy—I'm sitting here with one lady who's been in here biweekly for two and a half years, one who's on her second treatment and still learning the ropes, and one who has just completed her treatment, only to find out that it hasn't worked. All appear strong and all are smiling! Smiling, even though the treatment didn't work. That's faith, faith to believe God is at work, whether our thoughts differ from His as to how this should end. Less of the shadows, more of the sun, less of the battles, more victories to come, over and over, time and again, God will be faithful!

August 28, 2008—day four of chemotherapy—I was told to expect the worst between days one and four after my treatment, so I chose to wait and give everyone an update tonight. On Monday, Jeff and I went to the oncology clinic and had my first round of two of my chemotherapy drugs administered. I experienced a slight headache and a few waves of nausea, but otherwise did pretty well. On Tuesday we went back for the third drug (they administer them at different times so they can be alerted to any reaction that may occur). About an hour after the treatment, I felt several waves of nausea, a headache, and some chills and fever, and decided it would be best to lie down as soon as I got home. After several hours of chills and fever, it passed and I felt a little more like myself. On day three I awoke at 7:30 a.m., began washing clothes, working in the office, and then I walked a mile on the elliptical. I had an enormous amount of energy and prepared for the weekend. Tonight we sang in Richmond, IN. It was a very warm congregation and everyone was so kind. I told Jeff I wanted to sing every opportunity that God gave me, and I'm very grateful for each one.

One of my favorite funny stories happened one night during a Gaither Homecoming concert. Typically, just before we walk onstage, Jeff would be positioned to one side of the stage and I would be on the opposite. We would then walk to each other center stage and begin singing. My dear friend Janet Paschal had been such an inspiration throughout breast cancer along with my Aunt Janis, who had breast cancer twice. It was these two ladies who I turned to for all of my breast cancer related questions. One night Janet offered to give me a pair of false eyelashes. By this time my hair had thinned and I had lost all of my eyebrows and eyelashes and was just learning how to put myself together for the stage. I put the eyelashes on, and as Jeff tells the story, we met onstage and all he could see was eyelashes. It reminded him of one of his favorite childhood movies, *Rudolph, the Red-Nosed Reindeer*, when Rudolph meets his girlfriend Clarice!

September 24, 2008—Round two, day ten—I'm doing extremely well with the chemo. I haven't had to take any anti-nausea medication, my energy level is great, and my blood counts were so good with the first round my doctor doesn't have to see me until round three! Praise God for the many prayers that are being offered on my behalf....I still have my hair, although my hairdresser gave me a really short, easy to take care of "do" last Thursday! Monday, our family attended a presentation by our county and the Georgia Department of Transportation to celebrate the renaming of the road on which we live to the "James Roy 'Pop' Lewis Memorial Highway." What an honor! We were all so excited that Pop was being memorialized in this manner. I was asked to be one of the speakers, and I couldn't help but point out that the most successful people I've ever known never set out to be great—they simply woke up each morning and made a lifetime of daily good and right choices which led to their success. Pop was a very humble man, never thinking of fame, simply thinking of the things that brought him joy—his family and his music. These joys and his uncanny ability to have a response to any question ever posed, usually with humor, garnered him his legacy. I'm so proud to be the granddaughter of a man who was so loved by so many!

October 18, 2008—Round three, day thirteen—Jeff said something the other day that reminded me of an article I read just after my diagnosis in July. We were on our way home from a quick trip to Augusta, and he said, "You know, this really hasn't been so bad." I assume he saw daggers lunge from my eyes by the way he reacted, but instead of being angry I laughed, no I guffawed! It was hysterically funny to me! After all the queasiness, the fatigue, the emotional and physical battle of surgery, the mourning of the gradual hair loss that worsens with every treatment, the nosebleeds, runny nose, sore throat, and you-name-it-and-it's-different symptoms that go on in your body because of chemo, I laughed a huge belly laugh. It reminded me of an article in our local paper written by one of my favorite local writers, Mickie McGee. The article was "things not to say to a cancer patient" and was really quite humorous. My favorite was "You have cancer? Is it bad?" To which you would reply, "Noooo, I've got the good kind!"

I'm typically an eternal optimist, and so I began thinking about the good things I've experienced in my life since July. Beginning with the diagnosis—we found it, many aren't so blessed. The surgery went well—thank God for great surgeons. A week after surgery, I had lost five pounds (hey, every woman gets excited about losing five pounds!) I received hundreds of cards, calls, etc., affirming that I was loved—although we should, we usually forget to tell each other this information without a reason. I had family and friends praying for me around the clock—another thing we should do more often and don't. At least if I lose all my hair, my brother is bald and if genetics play a part, I'll have a beautiful head! And wearing a wig assures me of the "best hair in the building" especially on a rainy night.

Looking at it this way makes me really glad I got the "good kind"!

October 25, 2008—I didn't get what I bargained for—I got more! Round four approaches and I am thinking about the unfairness of it all. I didn't do anything to deserve the cancer or the chemo and neither did Jeff or my kids. Yet rather than feel sorry for myself, I feel blessed.

December 13, 2008—The cumulative effects of chemo-therapy can wear a body down. Although it has been a difficult journey, God has been faithful and I am looking forward to a New Year with new beginnings! There have been days with tears, physical pain, and days so full of fatigue that I didn't even feel like getting out of bed. Still, through all of this, I was blessed never to miss a concert performance, but of course there were some days I slept until concert time, then returned to bed immediately afterwards.

My secret for surviving all of this—I haven't allowed chemo to rob me of my life. I told Jeff at the onset of the treatments, if I allow it, the chemo will rob me of all three of my children's birthdays, Halloween, Thanksgiving, and

Christmas—I refused! Instead, I found a rhythm and began to dance. I chose certain days to rest and do nothing, praying without ceasing and forcing myself to experience life on other days. My prayer for those of you facing long-term chemotherapy is to pace yourself. Train as if you are running a marathon, not a sprint. It's hard, very hard, but God is faithful.

On December 2, I was administered my last treatment. I expected to hear the "Hallelujah Chorus," but instead it was a quiet celebration among my newfound friends in the clinic. Today I feel wonderful, fully alive! I am very grateful for a cancer-free diagnosis and the end of chemotherapy. I now wait for my fingernails to become healthy again, eyelashes and eyebrows to grow, and although I never lost all my hair, it became very thin, and I wait anxiously for it to thicken. I continue to receive cards, calls, and gifts from encouragers everywhere, and for each of you I am so thankful. You have given me a spirit to fight when I didn't think I could. May God bless each of you bountifully for the giving of your hearts, and may you be blessed in your New Year of new beginnings!

February 22, 2009—It's been a lazy Sunday—I'm sitting here in the kitchen drinking a cup of hot tea. Jeff is working with his computer and projector; he's such a gadget guy.

Morgan has gone to bed because school comes early for her in the morning, while Maura sings and dances in the den as if she were performing for an audience of thousands. Madison has been living on his own for six months now but stopped by today to show me his new fascination, a black Lab puppy he just picked up today. I am grateful for each moment God blesses.

We just got back from a cruise to Mexico, and I feel so healthy with the return of my eyelashes and eyebrows! I've undergone another surgery in the reconstruction process, and I have a six-week checkup on Tuesday. I've scheduled bone scans and CT scans in March, and if all is well, I can have my port removed. It's been a very difficult eight months, and I'm looking forward to the time when I don't have a doctor's appointment on my calendar every week.

Throughout this battle I've heard so many stories from you, some very encouraging miracles, and some heart-wrenching losses. Life can be very difficult, but God is faithful! We're in the process of recording a new project, and it reflects many of the places we've found ourselves this year. I understand all too clearly these days the analogy of the mountain in physical and spiritual climbs, but one thing's for sure; you can't experience the view from the top if you never begin to climb."

June, 2009—How do you begin to describe what breathing in and out feels like, or what sunshine feels like on your skin, or how deep the red is in a rose? That's how I feel these days...really no words to describe my gratitude. It's bigger and better than words can tell. According to my second set of scans, the doctors say I'm still cancer-free, praise God. I feel great, my energy is returning, my hair is coming back with a vengeance, and I'm down to my last two surgeries. By the end of summer, I should be well on my way to being myself, which brings me to a great little story that happened to me recently. I was in a little shop in Gatlinburg, during Family Fest, and a couple there was trying to determine if I was in actuality Sheri Easter. When I got off the phone, the lady asked, "Are you Sheri?" and I replied, "Yes, I am." Her husband then responded with, "I knew it was you because I saw your scar." That little sentence became so profound to me by the end of the day. The scar that I try to hide, the one that reminds me of the chemotherapy and all the ugliness I went through last year...that scar told them who I was. I began to embrace the scar at the thought of the encouragement it could offer to others. Isn't that what this life of being a Christian is all about? Showing the world your scars so that they might be encouraged! Jesus wasn't ashamed to show Thomas His scars, neither was He bothered that

Thomas asked to see them. Embrace your scars, share them with others—your scars show the world who you are!

July 2, 2009—One year ago today, I received the most difficult news I've ever learned, the diagnosis of breast cancer, and today I am celebrating life. I had my final surgery ten days ago, and I'm feeling wonderful. Blessings to all of you who offered your prayers, calls, emails, and cards...they were my encouragement!

July 8, 2009—It's official...today is the anniversary of the removal of cancer from my body. I'm a survivor! I read somewhere that if you have ever been diagnosed with cancer, you are considered a survivor, but I kind of like counting from the day the cancer was officially removed. It seems to legitimize the title for me. At first I didn't like that word, "survivor." It felt a little too sickly or maybe even a little too boastful about not being sickly—whatever the reason, I have come to love the word, cherish its meaning in my life, and celebrate the title. I have a button, a ribbon, a tote bag, and a shirt that all proclaim my title....I am a survivor, one year and counting!

May 24, 2010—Today has been "another manic Monday," crazy and stressed, but ultimately blessed! Through eyes that see blessings, I watched a mother bird feed her babies

through my kitchen window and I cried. My son hugged me several times today, just because. Morgan's boisterous laugh fills the silence while Maura quietly plays a game on my iPad. Jeff hugs me all day to remind me everything will be okay, and I sit in the quiet now thanking God for good health, family, and lots of love.

July 15, 2010—I've just celebrated my two-year anniversary as a breast cancer survivor, and I am more assured today than ever before that God has a purpose for my life to encourage the lives of others. I've celebrated with other friends who have heard the words "cancer free," and I've mourned the loss of those who battled then rested in the arms of Jesus. Life can simply be overwhelming at times, but God is faithful. I feel stronger than I've felt in years, and I'm staying very busy with my family and travel schedule. With celebration as a theme, Jeff and I celebrated our 25th wedding anniversary June 18 and spent the evening with close friends and family just before we left for a family vacation to Disney World. We're going into the studio soon to record a couple of love songs that we are planning to add into a 25-song project entitled Silver to be released in January.

Personally, I am in the process of compiling some of my journaling from 1974 to the present, along with some of the songs I've written and many of the blogs written during those very dark days of breast cancer, because I found that I was most encouraged by hearing the stories of others who had fought hard and survived. I've always enjoyed writing of any nature and always had a desire to compile a book of my writings. So far it has been an interesting experience going back and reading some of the words I penned in my past. There were days that I could hear the joy bouncing off the pages, and days that I cried feeling losses all over again. It's amazing that just as a singer records emotion, a writer can pen emotion onto a page. That emotion can then express encouragement to others, offering hope to the hopeless and life to the lost. Now that's something to celebrate, so pardon me while I dance!

For a woman who makes her life's work communicating
essential messages, I could not even speak during the
darkest days of breast cancer.

—Sheri Easter

CHAPTER ELEVEN

Have a Heart

Our project *Expecting Good Things* is in essence a musical diary of my journey through breast cancer. It is our family's celebration of life! Each song told a story of hope, faith, and love. Below is a collection of blogs I wrote weekly to introduce the audiences to our new project prior to its release.

"Hear My Heart"

There is something very special about the quiet. It's the place where we hear God's voice most clearly, without the distractions of life. My life gets so busy with school functions, laundry, and doctor's appointments, feeding the dog, the cat and the fish, and a host of other necessary yet overwhelming chores. I long for understanding, for someone to know how I truly feel, but I simply don't have the time to express myself completely. The wonderful thing about God is that He only can hear your heart. Without words to get in the way, He knows just how you feel. That encourages me! "Hear My Heart" is a song I wrote with some friends of mine for our latest project...my prayer during the quietest time of my life!

"In the Name of Jesus"

Jeff recalls a time in his life when he was completely surrounded by fears. His daddy suggested that any time he felt oppressed, simply call on the name of Jesus. Jeff was a young teenager at the time but is still reminded of that every time he faces a fear. When we began reviewing songs for our new project, this song affirmed everything he had believed about the power in speaking the name of Jesus. According to the Word of God, we stand on the promise that at the mention of His name, demons will flee, hearts will be restored, and lives will be changed.

"I Don't Wanna Cry"

I can't think of anything more isolating than crying alone with no one to comfort you. As Christians, we are promised that God is always near, that He knows every teardrop that falls, and that He cares about the pain we endure. It's comforting to know that on your worst days—the days you feel like giving up—God knows you are hurting and He cares.

Remember this promise, "God will hold you when you cry wiping every tear from your eye."

"I Need You More Today"

When Morgan began singing with us, Jeff wanted to choose just the right song to showcase her voice, her presence, and most importantly her heart. We were on our way to an annual date in New Holland, PA, and Jeff was listening to the radio when this song recorded by The Bishops in the late eighties, early nineties began to play. The message was perfect, the melody was perfect, and there was no doubt it sounded like angels when the family harmonies began. We felt like the song was so relevant to what a fifteen-year-old would experience, and ironically the writer wasn't much older than that when she wrote the song. The song simply cries out to God for every need, because we are not self-sufficient, no matter how hard we try to convince ourselves we can go it alone. The truth is that we need Him, more today than yesterday!

"I Get To"

I remember hearing this song for the first time and thinking, "That just says it all!" We get into such a routine of living that we sometimes forget how to really live. We dread the chores, the deadlines, and even the expectations of others until we realize the blessing wrapped up in each one. Helping

Dad wash the car and cut the grass seems so mundane—until we realize that one day Dad might not be around. So instead of thinking I have to do something, we remember "I get to." With the awakening of life we experienced last year (2008), Jeff and I realize all too well that we don't have to do anything, we get to. It's become a motto of sorts around our house this year. These days we remind each other of all the wonderful things in life we "get" to do!

"Over the Mountain"

Last December our family took a trip to Disney World. It was just days before my final round of chemotherapy. When I got back to the bus that evening, I commented to Jeff as we were leaving the parking lot, "I may not be over the mountain, but I can see the other side." It's amazing how just a glimmer of hope can strengthen and carry you through the most difficult days of your life. It's all about perspective. I could see celebration in my near future; therefore, I prepared my spirit to celebrate. Keep your eyes on things that matter and you'll rise above the blue!

"Expecting Good Things"

Seems if we could just somehow find perspective and see "the big picture," we'd all do better at keeping a positive outlook on life. Too often we grumble and complain about minor inconveniences as if they were just the most horrible set of circumstances when in actuality they are just simply inconvenient. Paul said he had "learned to be content" in whatever state he found himself, meaning that we too can "learn to be content," trusting that God is at work in our lives. We really can trust Him with our every breath. Just because you can't see the sun doesn't mean it isn't there. Wake up each morning expecting good things, knowing that the sun will shine again, and believing that God and heaven are awaiting you!

"I Know I Love You"

There are a lot of things in life I don't know. Who invented the washing machine? Where is Timbuktu? Why have I been so blessed? And then there are those things I know beyond a shadow of a doubt. I know I love Jeff, and there is no sweeter sound than when he says my name. I know I fell in love with my babies the moment I held them in my arms and looked into their tiny eyes. I know that my mama can touch my hand and communicate things that words simply cannot. I may not know everything, but I know I am loved.

"Workin' on a Road"

At a Gaither concert, Gordon Mote approached Jeff with the idea that he should record the old Lester Flatt tune "Workin' on a Road." Jeff and I both remembered the song, and we began brainstorming ideas for how to give the old song new life. We were both brought up listening to bluegrass music, and the thing I think is so unique to bluegrass is the energy of the song. Whether the song is slow and mournful or chicken-pickin' fast, it exudes an energy that is captivating. Before long, you're tapping your toes or clapping your hands to a melody that feels like home. Nothing could have made this song any better than having our longtime friends and Grand Ole Opry members, Marty Stuart and Connie Smith, sing along with us. Also joining us on some really smooth bass is the new "voice" of WSM, Eddie Stubbs, a great friend of more than 25 years. Thanks to these legendary voices, the song, once again, became new!

"Love Remains"

After such a tough year, I told Jeff, "I hope and pray no one ever has to go through what we have, but I pray everyone can feel as loved." Cards, letters, phone calls, floral arrangements, small gifts, books, music, and emails—it was unbelievable to witness the outpouring of love from God's children. Prayers were being offered up on my behalf; my family was being lifted "into heavenly places" by these kind gestures. It's amazing when your solid ground is shaken, everything is stripped away, and your faith seems distant, the one thing that remains is love. "Satisfy us in the morning with your unfailing love, that we may sing for joy and be glad all our days"—Psalm 90:14 (NIV)

"Time for Me to Fly"

Last year (2008) as we began selecting songs for our upcoming project, the song "Time for Me to Fly" was the first song I chose, knowing that it would be the debut single for our daughter Morgan. She was accepting an awesome responsibility to travel and sing while still attending high school. I was very aware of the sacrifices she would have to make, but I also knew the overwhelming joy it would be to sing songs of hope and encouragement to a hurting world. Last year was a test of faith for our entire family, and Morgan knows firsthand how young people need encouragement when life doesn't seem fair. Spread your wings, baby girl, it's time for you to fly!

"Born to Climb"

Sometimes in life, the mountains we face overwhelm us at first sight, and we feel defeated before we ever begin the climb. Doubts creep in and cold, hard reality whispers, "That's impossible, you can't make it!" The truth is—you can't. The good news is—God can! Set your sights on God, knowing that He's working all things together for your good, knowing He loves you and has a purpose for your life, every day of it. Then trust Him. Remember that "grace has strengthened you time after time, so don't be afraid of the mountain, friend, you were born to climb."

"The Sun Will Shine Again"

Anniversaries require us to look back. I recently celebrated an anniversary I never planned to celebrate, the one-year anniversary of my initial diagnosis of breast cancer. Although I didn't plan it, I do celebrate. I celebrate being a survivor, and I've done an awful lot of looking back over the past month. I remember hurting so badly that falling asleep, when it rarely happened, was my only relief. I remember crying so much that there were no tears left to cry, just groans out of an aching heart. I remember anger, fear, and feeling like the unfairness of it all was simply more than I could bear. It was a dark time. A season without sunshine, nothing but clouds covering all my blue skies, but you know what else I remember? I remember the intimacy of God like I'd never known. I remember feeling so loved by family and friends that no words could adequately convey the depth. And I remember believing "the dark clouds will vanish and the rain will end, there's a brighter day around the bend, I know the sun will shine again."

Writers spend their lives trying to express their deepest
thoughts through poems, songs, stories, journal entries,
blogs, and even lists. They write because they have to.

—Sheri Easter

CHAPTER TWELVE

Know Me by Heart

Life is eager to teach us if we will allow it. I'm a note-taker. I make lists. That's how I begin a process of meditating over and committing to memory the things I learn. In life, we sometimes find ourselves frustrated because we can't find the words to express how we feel. It is in those times when words either won't come or won't convey what is in our hearts that we make feeble attempts to express ourselves. The gleaning process is what we learn from the experiences of life. When life happens, we must choose to learn from it. Here are a few of the truths I've gleaned from the people and things I love most:

God is my priority in life. I am grateful for the gift of His son, salvation, and eternal life. I was brought up in a God-fearing family whose "job" was to sing about the Lord's goodness and mercy to us all. I accepted Christ when I was eleven years old, but because I was so timid, I didn't profess that faith publicly until I was fifteen. At that time, I accepted a leadership position in my church as part of the worship team and, for a short time, as a Sunday school teacher for the preschool children.

My mama and daddy loved me deeply. Their lives have created mine, beyond DNA. I am my mama's child in my songs, my creativity, my devotion to my husband, and my nurturing spirit to my children. I am my daddy's child in my love for God's creation of nature, my curiosity, and my passion.

My husband, Jeff, has given me through his love a strength that I never knew I had. His kind heart challenges me to be kind. His generosity to others challenges me to give abundantly. Our songs have given me wings to soar when I didn't even know how to fly.

My children, Madison, Morgan, and Maura, have given me proof of love at first sight. Their faces make me smile. Their words make me laugh.

My family is a simple tree with roots that run deep. There is a deep respect and love among its branches. They flourish with God's love. They are good people.

My friends have taught me about trust and compassion. They have shared my burdens and carried them when I was too weak to carry them alone.

My peers have challenged me to hone my craft and to persevere when I felt defeated. They have filled me when I was empty.

Songs have taught me how to worship from my heart. It is a gift to have been reared in a house filled with music.

Getting to know yourself may be one of the most important things you will ever do. Not all of us are basketball stars, teachers, or dancers, but if you take the time to discover what makes you happy, you're on to something great. Find out what makes you happy and pursue it. Do you like to sing? Sing in nursing homes, at church, or anywhere you can. Do you enjoy working with children? Offer to help with a Sunday school class. My friend Andy Andrews says there may not be a job available, but there's always work to be done—do something! By doing something, you will find value in and purpose for your life. It's been said that if you do things you love, you'll never work a day in your life. Do something you love and you will discover who you are. God has equipped you with all that you need to be the person He has called you to be.

I remember a time early in our marriage when Jeff and I were having a discussion about something, and suddenly he asked, "Why do you have to be so opinionated?" To which I replied, "I'm not opiona...so what's wrong with being opinionated? At least I know what I believe!" That simple comment helped me to understand myself a little better. Discovering your strengths and weaknesses will help you make peace with your shortcomings, and you'll not only learn to love yourself, but love others as well.

As in everything in life, we must be willing to fail in order to achieve success. In order to sing well, we must risk singing badly. Don't ever be afraid to try. Offer an expression of your heart and risk that it will result in success.

Sometimes we must make peace with the woman
in the mirror. She is not always a true reflection
of who we really are.

—Sheri Easter

I've always had aspirations of doing great things. I was the kind of kid who enrolled in everything from debate teams to beauty pageants, business organizations to social clubs. I love being involved, and thus the hardest lesson for me to learn is the one about filling your plate with too much of the unimportant—I'm a Martha! I tend to be so busy that I sometimes miss what's important. I have a difficult time resting. It is in my nature to be busy 24/7, nonstop. Therefore, when I lie down at night, my mind begins to dance—things to do, things to say, things to write, things in general. I am a worker, a doer; it is where I am at my best! In all honesty, though, a person cannot work or do unless he first learns to be! Many times I have made a conscious choice to be...a wife, a mom, a daughter, a sister, or a friend. These titles make up my being so that I may do the things that God gives me the opportunity to do.

As a singer and songwriter, I'm always searching for a way to relate to my audience. The one thing that seems to permeate all genres of music, all denominations of religions, and all classes of society is love. Every one of us, no matter how rich or poor, male or female, black or white—we all want and need to be loved. It is the tie that binds. I can remember from an early age desiring to be a good wife and mother, and those two jobs are always at the top of my list of priorities because I realize their eternal value. I am a mom who spends her whole day juggling, hoping that when the goodnight kisses are passed out, I have accomplished more than just the daily tasks.

It has been said that the majority of cards mailed from prison are sent to someone's mother. Almost everyone wants to let "Mama" know just how special she is. If we are fortunate to have had a good mother, it is a treasure. If not, it is something we long for our entire lives.

A few years ago I heard a speaker ask a profound question that caused me to look a little closer in the mirror—a little more deeply than I had looked before. He asked, "If you were to die today, what would you want people to say about you?" I thought long and hard about my answer. I thought of many admirable traits for which I'd love to be remembered—she was a good wife to her husband, a good mother to her children, she sang songs that made a difference in people's lives, she loved God. All of these ideas are good and admirable, but I wanted to condense it into what was most important to me. I came up with two very simple words that I believe say it all: She loved. If someone were to pass by my graveside a hundred years from now and read those two words engraved in stone, they'd know all they would ever need to know about me.

But we have the mind of Christ and do hold

the thoughts of His heart.

1 Corinthians 2:16 (AMP)

I love the analogy of metals being purified by fire in describing how the pain you endure in life brings out the character of who you are. It has been said that the things you learn in life are almost always taught in times of suffering. I know it has been true in my life. During my battle with breast cancer, I understood early that this tragedy would soon become something for which I would be truly grateful. I addressed the issue of suffering in a recent article.

Born of Suffering

I've always been little. Five-foot-nothing. I weighed 95 pounds on my wedding day and wear a pinkie ring, size 1 1/2. Never my idea of what the word "strong" would conjure up. Yet I realized in adulthood that strength was one of my most identifiable traits.

I had never thought of myself as strong. I don't ride amusement park rides, I don't watch scary movies, I really don't do anything that seems "brave." So when we had a time of devotion at one of our Homecoming concerts, I was surprised by an exercise that would later carry me through the darkest time of my life.

When I was 20, my daddy died of a sudden heart attack. I was a junior in college and my world was flipped upside down. I was devastated. Like it or not, I became an adult very quickly and began helping my mama make all of the decisions that adults have to make...funeral arrangements, insurance changes, legal documentation choices, etc. I never witnessed the change, it simply happened.

Four years before I was diagnosed with breast cancer, at one of the concerts during devotions, Anthony Burger's wife LuAnn gave us an "assignment." We were to attach two bookmarks to our backs with safety pins, then walk around and write anonymously a one- or two-word description of the person whose cards you were signing. We later read our cards, realizing that we don't always see ourselves as others see us. I was so surprised to read words like "strong woman of God," "strength," and "strongest person I know" because I simply didn't see myself that way.

In 2008, after the diagnosis that turned my world upside down, I opened my Bible and those bookmarks fell out. I read those words and cried uncontrollably. The suffering I experienced through my daddy's death had made me a woman of strength, a woman equipped to fight, a woman who was determined to be victorious, a woman who refused to give up. It made me...a survivor!

I've decided since I came through breast cancer that everyone in my audience is in one of three places. One, they are in the best times of their lives, with no heartache to bring them down. Two, they are in the middle of the worst days of their lives and barely find the strength to get out of bed. Or three, they have just come through the greatest tragedy of their lives and are celebrating the blessings with eyes wide open. Regardless of where you are right now, we all share a unified trait. We can all find something for which to be grateful. Gratitude is a concept that unites.

Not that I speak in respect of want: for I have learned, in whatsoever state I am, therewith to be content.

Philippians 4:11 (KJV)

CHAPTER THIRTEEN

Heart of the Matter

Through the years, I've been asked to write pieces for different magazines on many different subjects. Here is a compilation of my thoughts written over the past twenty years, beginning with and in honor of mothers:

My first Mother's Day was in 1989. Madison was almost six months old, so the gift giving was in Jeff's hands. He asked me what I wanted and was a little surprised when I replied, "A vacuum cleaner!" It just seemed so "motherly." Since that time my most memorable Mother's Day gifts have been the dinners together, the handmade crafts from school, and the hugs and kisses all week long. I'm so glad there's a Mother's Day...I need to call Mama!

This one was unique in that they wanted the article to be "Like Mother, Like Daughter, Like Daughter, Like Daughter," trailing the relationships of Grandma, Mama, me, then Morgan. Here is the article written from my perspective:

Mama feels like she missed out on a lot of events and says she regrets it very much, however, from my little brother's perspective and mine, we never felt neglected in any way. From our point of view, she compensated for her absence, over and above what was necessary by giving us quality time. She was at home every Monday through Thursday, and it felt as if she was an "at-home" mom. She made all the school activity errands, baked cookies for meetings, had time for my friends to come over, and, believe me, with a kid like me, she had her work cut out for her. I was into every club, meeting, activity, etc., that I could be in, and I kept her busy. We were very proud of her talent and her fame as a singer. She wasn't "away," she was just special.

Mama is everything I've always wanted to be. She's beautiful, talented, a good businesswoman, kind, thoughtful, compassionate, and a wonderful wife of almost twenty-five years to my daddy (after Daddy's death, she remarried and is also a good wife to Leon). She's a terrific mom, godly, moral, and every good adjective I can think of. I've often described her as an angel without wings! She's never had a bad day, always perky (her grandfather called her "sunshine"), and she used to get spankings for giggling…see why I'd like to be like her?

It always impressed me that Mama was always available to do whatever I needed, whenever I needed it done, no matter how busy her schedule. If ever I had gotten to school and forgotten something, I could call her knowing she hadn't been home but a few hours and probably hadn't gotten ready for the day, and I could ask her to bring something for me. Without hesitation, she'd bring it to the school, smiling and grateful to help. She worked at my grandma's in the office two to three hours each day, and when I'd get in from school, she'd been putting up groceries, wondering what we'd like for supper. This is the amazing part that I still don't have figured out! She traveled all weekend, worked in the office every weekday, ran all our errands, and still cooked a full meal every night, "meat and three"! I don't know how she did it. I keep the same schedule and my kids ask for Ravioli!

When I became a mom, it changed everything! How I packed, how much time it took to get from point A to point B, and how I made decisions. Our booking agent will call and pitch a date, and many times I will turn it down because of Morgan's dance recital or because it's not a school holiday. It's tricky to balance the two worlds, but I do a lot of what I learned from Mama. The paperwork is done during school hours, and the arrangement of our dates is determined by their school schedule.

I feel privileged to have had the heritage I have. My grandma was a preacher's daughter, always reading her Bible, always praying. My mama carried her love for God along with a smile, and when you have women like that guiding your life, you know you're in good hands.

Character is who you are when no one but God is watching.

—Unknown

This is a story I wrote from third-person perspective about my baby girl, Maura, and myself. She loved for me to read to her, and to this day she has a love for books like me. It always intrigues me when I look at my children and see a reflection of me—good or bad, it's like finding a part of you that you may have long forgotten.

For the Love of Words

"Once upon a time," she began as she had hundreds of times before. Mama didn't need to look at the pages, for by now it was inscribed on the pages of her heart. What was so special about this book? she wondered. Was it the story itself? Maybe it was the pretty colored pictures…or the way Mama's voice rose high and then scaled down low. It could be the rhythmic vibrations coming from Mama's chest. The more she thought about it, she began to realize that it wasn't the book, or the pretty pictures, the sound of her voice, or the hum of the rhythmic vibrations she felt. What was so special for Baby Maura was the moment itself. THIS moment. No, it wasn't the book; it was the simple fact that for Baby Maura and Mama this moment belonged to the two of them.

This is an article about an ordinary life:

I started thinking one day how sometimes the extraordinary comes disguised in ordinary clothing. My first thought was my marriage. To others it may appear very ordinary, but to us it's quite extraordinary. It may seem that we get up, get the children ready for school, scramble out the door with no time to spare, make phone calls, pay the bills, repair what needs repairing, pick up the children, drop them off at piano or dance, pick them up, then fall into bed around midnight! On the surface, that's exactly what it is, but underneath there is a deep love, respect, admiration, friendship, and a bonding that occurs every day during those mindless tasks. It's the same way with God's handiwork. It comes to us disguised and seeming so ordinary—like that unexpected song on the radio that lifts and encourages, the check in the mail that blesses, or the negative test results from the doctor's office. These seem so ordinary, yet they affect us in extraordinary ways by saying, "God is here, He is with us." I sometimes wonder what Mary's day was like just before the angel appeared. Was she washing clothes, cleaning the house? And just before she delivered her baby, was she resting from her journey, having supper, worrying about her future? We know she was on her way to register to pay her taxes—that seems pretty ordinary. The day I accepted Christ as my personal Savior, no bells sounded, no parade came through our tiny little town, no horns or confetti…just a simple ordinary message that left my heart pounding and began in my life an extraordinary experience.

October 11, 1999—It is a very special moment when you realize God is speaking. Last night, I was awakened by a disturbing dream about Jeff. I knew because of back trouble he had gone into the hotel around 4 a.m. It was now 6:30 a.m. and I was so afraid of waking him, nevertheless, my uneasiness wouldn't allow me to sleep. I rummaged through the briefcase and located the number of the hotel. I asked that they ring Jeff Easter's room, and I heard that sweet familiar "Hello." It was a warm embrace. We talked a few minutes, said "I love you" like when we were dating, and hung up. I went back to my bed with a peace. I felt a need to read a scripture, and since Gloria Gaither had mentioned the book of Song of Solomon in the latest video, I decided I'd dip back into that scripture of love. As I began to read chapter 3, verse 1, I realized I was being spoken to by the Almighty. I wasn't the first lover who was awakened in the night with concern for her beloved. God allowed me to see what a precious gift I had in my "best friend" and to cherish a moment from our dating years. I haven't seen him yet, he's on his way to pick us up, but I'm sure I'll be like the Shulamite woman when she saw her beloved. "I held him and would not let him go..." (NIV). Thank You God for reminding me that every minute spent with my beloved is a "precious and rare jewel to be treasured." Never should time between a wife and a husband be mundane or undesirable. It should be treated as an honor and a privilege. Thank You God for this privilege.

Celebrating our twenty-fifth, our silver anniversary, was very special. We chose twenty-three of our favorite love songs from previous recordings and recorded two new songs that we each loved. Our children joined us for the harmonies, Madison singing Jeff's song and Morgan singing mine, and it was a beautiful celebration for our family. Here are the liner notes I wrote in order to commemorate this occasion:

Twenty-five years. Marriage vows, hand me downs, and a lot of love. Baby bottles, report cards, dance lessons, "Are we there yets?" Video games, guitars, graduation, and a lot of love. Science projects, toys, cheerleading, and a piano. Disney World, surprise baby number three, breast cancer, aging parents, and a lot of love. Tears, bicycles, laughter, braces, and suddenly another walk down the aisle approaches. This expedition called life is full. It is rich. It is a daily commitment to love, honor, and respect those who share your journey. Twenty-five years with God's abundant blessings and a lot of love!

Below is an article I wrote regarding my New Year's resolution for 2001. It's nice to look back and, with words, remember the spiritual and emotional places we've been.

I recently finished reading a book, *The Prayer of Jabez*. It explained why Jabez was so blessed, in fact so blessed that he was described in 1 Chronicles 4:9 as "more honorable than his brothers." In verse 10, we discover why—the prayer of his heart, the prayer of Jabez. "Oh that you would bless me indeed and enlarge my territory, that your hand would be with me, and that you would keep me from evil, that I may not cause pain." The desire of Jabez was to do more and be more for God. That's my New Year's resolution and my desire for 2001. If we can do more and be more for God, we can do more and be more for our families, our friends, and our associates.

It might be nice if we always had the advantage of hindsight. Maybe it could spare us some of the pain we inflict on those we love most as well as ourselves. As I re-read my own words and this prayer that I sincerely prayed for this upcoming New Year, I can now look back and see that God was faithful. He enlarged my territory by taking me into several foreign countries I had never been able to visit before. His hand was with me and I was kept from evil. So often we worry and fret about things that will never come to pass.

How much more blessed would we be if we truly trusted Him to lead us down each pathway, open each door, and believe in His ability to enlarge our territory. Our desire should always be rooted in being and doing more for God. He'll take care of the rest!

Quote for New Year 2002

I resolve to love more, stronger, greater, more often, and deeper each day. For love sustains when life is hard.

I'm so busy, I don't know if I found a rope or lost a horse.

—Unknown

I was writing a journal entry today in one of those "your life in your own words" journals for my children. The entry question for today was, "Tell me about your best childhood friend." As I began to describe her, I found myself noting how very much alike we are. We are both pretty easygoing, extremely dependable, responsible, organized, detailed, over-achieving perfectionists who find joy in seeing how much we can get accomplished in a day. We had excellent grades, were members of every club we could qualify for, competed in all the local beauty pageants and programs, and volunteered for service work at the senior citizens' program and junior organizations in our free time.

We are "Marthas," and the truth of the matter is that Marthas are good, as long as they remember to stop achieving long enough to listen to the words of Christ. I called my friend today and we laughed about what an incredible resume we have to offer, yet who remembers, and even if they did, is that what we'd want them to remember? Or would we prefer they remember that we listened and loved?

I was also the kind of kid who waited in line at the water fountain while several others broke in line ahead of me. I never said anything, yet when I think about that now, as an adult, you begin to realize that life is not always fair. It is filled with unfairness sometimes. You grow into the place where you realize that the attitude, the joy, the peace all have to come from inside and not from the people or circumstances surrounding you. You discover that some things are worth fighting for and other things aren't worth the effort. You discover what is important and what is not.

Life can be busy, life can be unfair, and it can overwhelm you at times; nevertheless, you are in control of your responses to whatever life sends your way. Find in Christ a deep-seated joy that will sustain you through the busyness and unfairness of life. Find a perspective that allows you to see your blessings instead of your lack.

I'd like to think that I have all the answers, the ability to do all the right things, and the stamina to get everything accomplished in a timely manner; however, the truth is most days I don't have a clue. I don't really know how to be a good wife, good mother, good friend, or good businesswoman. I simply wake up, pray for God's guidance, and trust Him to do the rest. It's funny; I've just reminded myself of my greatest character trait...the ability to recognize that I am nothing without Christ. Praise God, the pressure's off!

Remembering who you are in Christ makes all the difference. I've been afforded the opportunity to work with some wonderfully talented people through the years, but it's when I begin to see the heart, the place where Christ resides, that's when my heart makes a true friend. In gospel music, we lost two dear friends within six days of each other. Our loss is truly heaven's gain.

Vestal was a legend to so many people, and I guess I never realized until the past ten years or so, simply because I'd always thought of her as a friend. I can't say for certain when I first met The Goodmans, but years before I was born they became friends to my family by opening doors to have them perform along with them in concerts here in the South. Rusty and JD Sumner were the first to put my uncle, Little Roy, on stage when he was just a child. Rusty was known as "Charlie" to my folks, but I'm not sure why. All the Goodmans were common names in our household including Vestal. For years, I'd see her at all the concerts backstage, and she was always so good to me. I felt certain she'd picked me out of all the others to fuss over. When Jeff and I first began traveling, we would always mention whenever we'd see someone who looked like Vestal, and of course, in that day there were many who emulated her. One Sunday we performed at a concert about five miles from where Howard and Vestal lived, and Jeff whispered to me onstage, "Vestal's here." I expected to see someone who looked like Vestal. I couldn't believe it when I looked about halfway back of the congregation and Vestal waved at me. We called her up onstage to sing one with us, and she told the audience that in her car was one cassette and it was Jeff and Sheri! She was very serious and proved it to us later that evening. When Bill began his videos, we were able to work side by side with her nightly, and during the filming of the *Homecoming Kids* videos, our son Madison fell in love with her and she with him. She'd always want to know where my children were and what they were doing. She sent them her love, here latest CDs, and sometimes her homemade goodies. I was honored to record with her on several occasions, and it was always a treat to harmonize with her. She sang from her heart, and you knew it when you sang with her. Many times I've sat beside her on stage and she'd pass me her handkerchief when she'd see me crying. I always offered them back, but she insisted that I keep them. I have one framed in my office with a personal handwritten note, "Especially for Sheri." I've put one up for each of my children for keepsakes. I've shared some of my greatest heartaches with Vestal, and each time she listened to every detail and began to pray. Vestal made me feel as if she truly picked me out above all others. She prayed for me. I will deeply miss my friend, Vestal.

Jeff and I just returned from our trip to Columbus, Georgia, where we said our goodbyes to our dear friend, Jake Hess. I believe it was the kind of goodbye Jake would have wanted—common, touchable, gentle, and endearing, kind of like a walk down memory lane. Bill mentioned how Jake was the kind of person who didn't worry about tomorrow or fret over the past. He simply lived for today with fondness of the past and an optimistic hope for tomorrow. I've known Jake since I was just a little girl from the concerts my family shared with him. He and Hovie were dear to my family, and there seemed to always be a common love and respect between these southern gospel Georgia artists. As an adult, the first time I had the opportunity to share the stage with Jake was at an awards presentation. I commented to him that it was such an honor to be presenting with him, to which he cordially replied, "No, the honor is mine." The last time I shared the stage with him was at the T.D. Jakes filming where we sang "Sweeter As the Days Go By" together with Joy Gardner, David Phelps, and Mike Allen. Jake left our tour in the spring of 2003 due to health complications, yet he never left our hearts. We continued to call or write from time to time to let him know how terribly he was missed. Jake truly was a "gentle" man. I'm not sure that I've ever met anyone quite like him. If you knew Jake, surely you loved him. He always had a response, whether witty or sincere, to every situation he encountered.... something I'd refer to as a very special gift. One of my favorite Jake stories, and we do have many, was the night we were on stage for the homecoming portion of the concert. Jake and I were sitting together, and Jeff was to the left of me. You must understand that among artists, Jeff's "quartet tenor voice" is infamously obnoxious, and he loves to sing it HIGH and LOUD! This particular night, Jeff was trying to impress Jake with his natural gift, and Jake leaned over to me and said, "Maybe if we ignore him, he'll go away!" I laughed and replied, "No, Jake, I've been ignoring him for eighteen years and he's still here!" Then, of course, there were the many occasions when Jeff would start rubbing Jake's arm saying, "Jake, you don't mind do you? I've never rubbed a legend before!" Once Jeff was telling Jake the story of how we had given Hovie a ride home and he'd left his cap, the one he'd worn in many videos and performances. When Jeff offered to mail it back to him, Hovie told Jeff to keep it for the kindness that our family extended to him bringing him home. As Jeff was proudly telling this story to Jake, Jake reminded him that he'd never asked him for his hair! Immediately Jeff asked, to which Jake replied, "I'll bring you the one that hangs on the back of my closet door and scares me every time I open it." Jake was true to his word, and today in our office we keep Jake's hair, Hovie's cap, and Vestal's hankie, and we smile every time we pass by. The last time we saw Jake was very much like the first. He was always kind, sincere, humble, and smiling with unusual optimism. When asked, "How are you doing, Jake?" his reply was always, "Nothin' but fine, nothin' but fine." I sincerely believe if we could ask him that same question now, we'd hear his same reply, "Nothin' but fine."

CHAPTER FOURTEEN

Wholehearted

Words have helped me express my heart throughout my life, and I have a deep appreciation for honest communication. Shallow, superficial conversation, although it never rubs you wrong, also never leaves a lasting impression. We have a favorite phrase for that kind of communication. "Great hair, hope you win!" may lift you for a moment, but it doesn't offer anything that sustains. Like it or not, truth and honesty help to shape a person.

With the passing of my daddy at such an early age, I have spent my lifetime seeking out friends who would open themselves up to me in truth and honesty because of the deep intimacy that can be brought out only by hearing another's pain. In today's society so many people are blaming others for their failures when in actuality they have not yet been honest with themselves. I could always count on honesty from Mama and Daddy. I could count on honesty from my grandparents. I can count on honesty from my husband and my children, but rare are the friends who tell it like it is! Cherish those friendships where deep and true communication abides. God has blessed you with those very special people.

The Bible tells us that God knows what we need before we ask or think to ask. He alone knows what is in our hearts. He is a friend in whom we can confide. He knows our faults, our character flaws, our bad habits, and He is still head over heels in love with us. We can be honest with Him, knowing that we need not explain; we simply need to acknowledge our neediness for Him and all He has to give us. The very special relationship we have with God requires that no words be spoken; just offer Him an honest heart.

I love it when I've developed such an intimacy with someone that only a look can say everything that needs to be spoken. That's honest communication. That's truth. That's intimacy at its deepest level. That's the kind of love that leaves you satisfied.

Don't use words too big for the subject. Don't say "infinitely" when you mean "very"; otherwise you'll have no word left when you want to talk about something really infinite.

—C. S. Lewis

Words

I've always had a love/hate relationship with words. Some words make me want to dance, and others frustrate me to no end. A writer is always trying to express what's in the heart. The frustration is that there really are no words sharp enough, smart enough, smooth enough, or soft enough to convey what is in our hearts. So we begin our futile attempts to express what's inside by sorting through the piles of words stored in our heads to find just the right ones to put on paper so the reader can understand how we feel. It is a writer's desire to be able to write what the heart feels.

My life began with the words "buffly," "da-da," and "ma-ma." "Buffly" because of the mobile suspended above my crib, and "da-da" and "ma-ma" for obvious reasons. I love words and their ability to make people laugh, cry, heal, hope, comfort, and love. The written word became a large part of my life at an early age. My mama read to me often and remarked to friends that she had become "book poor" after buying literally hundreds of books for my little brother and me. I still have all my books and more. I am now officially "book poor." I love the way they look, the way they feel, the way they transport me to faraway places and times, and the way they help me to gain perspective. I buy books for my children, my family, my friends, and even folks who may not read. I figure if a book makes me so happy, surely they need to know this joy too.

Mama says I began writing notes in kindergarten with a "B" or "P" reminding me to bring my "book" or "paper" since I had no idea how to spell at that age. Every day I make a list, and everything that transpires in my day relates back to what the list dictates. Of course, as the items are done, each line is dutifully scratched out. Some days the list says exactly the same thing as the day before. The list includes "to-do" items, "don't forget" items, phone numbers to call, spring cleaning notes, "I love you's," and "to pack" items. My husband teases that I need to add his name to the list some days.

My children are so used to seeing my Post-it notes or lists that they don't even notice them anymore. If I'm not at home when I should be, they know to look for my note, otherwise it blends into the countertop. Through the years, my children have written notes because they wanted to remember something important. I still have those notes, and one day I'll pull them out to remind them of how words have filled both my life and theirs.

Books teach me knowledge, experience

teaches me wisdom.

—Unknown

This is from an article I wrote about the love of reading. I still count reading as one of my favorite guilty pleasures.

I love to read. I typically keep 3-4 books in several locations and read them all simultaneously. Some of my favorite books would be:

My Bible, King James Version is my favorite because of the poetry in the writing. I keep several in the house and on the bus for convenience. When I travel, it's so important to me to pack a Bible for the encouragement it offers. Many times I've been on a plane and slightly anxious about a long flight ahead of me. Immediately, I open my Bible for the encouragement in the Scriptures about how God is with me wherever I am and that He hasn't given me a spirit of fear. He goes before me, and it lifts me to be reminded. I also face the same stresses and trials that others face, and it helps to calm the tendency to worry. When my daddy passed away suddenly of a heart attack, my Bible was a constant source of encouragement. No other time in my life before or since have I so desperately searched the Scriptures for answers. The Psalms offered David's anger and similar forsakenness that I was feeling at the time, and it helped me to know that I could, in honesty, cry out to God for His comfort and leading.

Gone with the Wind has been my favorite for many years. As a Southern girl, I can relate to many of the landscape descriptions, plus have you ever known any villain you can love as much as Scarlett? I've read this one several times through, all 1,036 pages, and still read it as though it's brand new to me. Each time I read it, I fall in love again with Scarlett and Rhett. In my mind, I have the luxury to add to Ms. Mitchell's story and assure myself that Rhett doesn't really leave and that Scarlett won't have to worry that "tomorrow is another day." For this is the beauty of a great love story with an open ending.

Any books that have been written by Max Lucado will find a place on my top favorites. One in particular that comes to mind is *In the Grip of Grace*. I carried this one on vacation one year when we took a family trip to Cancun, Mexico. I was out by the pool with the children when I read the chapter about Jeffrey Dahmer. In this chapter, Lucado parallels his life to Dahmer's, basically stating that grace is grace for anyone who receives. It is not earned or merited, it is simply extended. I, like Max, found a moment of pride that tried to convince me it couldn't possibly be. Then I reexamined and admitted that, yes, grace is grace to all. There are no limits or exclusionary terms, and there was nothing I had or hadn't done to merit God's grace. It was extremely liberating to know that I would be loved and extended grace simply because of God's choosing.

CHAPTER FIFTEEN

Heavy Heart

Several years ago, my sweet Mama was diagnosed with Parkinson's disease and Lewy body dementia. We had begun to notice that she would repeat stories as if she were telling them for the first time, and she had all but lost her sense of smell. I asked her to go to the doctor, and she admitted that she was afraid of finding out it might be something bad. Her brother, Wallace, had been diagnosed with Parkinson's and was slowly losing his ability to do anything without assistance. Because of his diagnosis, she was afraid. Reluctantly, she agreed to see a specialist and was later diagnosed.

As soon as we received the news, we felt responsible for letting her music fans know because she was concerned that she might not behave like herself and wanted to be open and honest about her condition. The following is a letter I posted on our websites:

An Open Letter to Fans & Friends

It is with a heavy heart I write these words to all of you who have supported my mama, Polly, and The Lewis Family for many years. A few days ago, Mama was diagnosed with Parkinson's disease, plus Lewy body dementia. While Parkinson's typically affects motor skills, over 50% of Parkinson's patients develop Parkinson's disease dementia (PDD), which is a Lewy body dementia that affects cognitive skills by disrupting perception, thinking, and behavior. By the symptoms Mama is experiencing, we are told that she is in the very early stages. She has begun medication and we are hopeful because of the early diagnosis. It is important to Mama that all of you know so that your prayers would be with her in the years ahead as she continues traveling. I'm certain that all of you who have ever met her are fully aware of why her grandfather called her "Sunshine." If you were fortunate enough to meet her, you also know that she never forgot a face or a name. While everything inside me wants to scream out that life isn't fair, I am quietly stilled by the message that each of our families has sung about through the years. God is faithful and is an ever-present help in our time of need.

Mama is committed to the music and to the fans, just as her daddy, mama, and brother were committed for so many years. She plans to continue her regular touring schedule of 100,000 miles annually for as many years as God allows and is looking forward to seeing each of you through her travels. Please pray for Mama. We love and deeply appreciate all of you for your concern and continued prayers.

Mama continued to travel until the fall of 2009, and in November of that year, after fifty-eight years of touring, The Lewis Family retired. During those final months of concerts, she continued to emcee the program and sing all the songs. At one concert in particular, she began to explain that she was ill and told the audience, "I've been diagnosed with, uh, uh…Janis [directing her question to her younger sister], what have I been diagnosed with?" Janis quickly replied, "Dementia," and the entire audience laughed along with them. My family has always been able to laugh. Shortly after her diagnosis, I was asked to write a piece for a magazine for Mother's Day.

I am the woman I am because of Mama. A loving, devoted, gentle yet strong, Southern woman, my mama has been an incredible example for me. Though many would cite her soulful voice as her greatest attribute, she will be quick to tell you that her children are her greatest achievements. She is a gifted businesswoman and the greatest communicator I've ever known. She was married to my daddy for 24 years until his sudden death in 1984. She became a widow at 47 years of age and continued to raise my younger brother and me on a single income. She was gifted at stretching a dollar and was able to put me through college for my last year without a complaint. When my daddy died, I became the person she depended on for advice in home matters and soon found her to be, not only my mama, but also my closest friend. In January, she celebrated her 70th birthday and was recently diagnosed with Parkinson's disease and Lewy body dementia. The communication we have always had is becoming somewhat strained, and now requires a bit more repetition, yet it is equally as kind and gentle as ever. Most days it is as though nothing has changed—those are my favorite days. She still continues to travel and sing 100,000 miles each year and works with her hands in business and household duties as she always has. Her beautiful smile is still what gets me through the toughest moments of my life.

As I retype these words, my heart aches for that time of "somewhat strained communication." These days are very different. She now depends on us for everything—feeding, bathing, walking, and her communication is so impaired that we celebrate the tiny sentences like "I love you too." Jeff and I are privileged to put her to bed each night when we're home. When life gives you new music, you must learn to dance and that we have. He takes her by the arms as I take her legs, and we carefully move to the new rhythm of putting her into bed. Afterward, we like to tell stories and sing songs. Because singing and speaking come from two different parts of the brain, she is still able to sing harmony with us on old favorites like "In the Sweet By and By" or "One Day at a Time." She always has a smile for us, and it is Jeff's job to make her laugh.

Recently we were putting her in bed and Jeff got down really close to her face and began his comedic routine, "Hey, Polly, do you know who this is?" She quickly replied, "You need to brush your teeth," and we celebrated—we had an entire sentence!

With the disease, we've learned to accept each day as it is, good or bad, and we are grateful for the good days. Her husband of eighteen years, Leon, is always by her side, and it is his "job" to be her caregiver. Leon, who is now approaching eighty, also has help in the home, and we recently brought in hospice to aid. We are blessed to celebrate every moment and make good memories along the way.

Recently my son went with me to visit my precious mama, and she struggled with her words until she finally stopped mid-sentence and began to cry. I took her hand and asked, "Mama, are you trying to say that you're proud of Madison and that you love him?" She nodded, and I assured her that she didn't have to ever worry about communicating that to any of us because of how well she has communicated that all through the years. We already know how much she loves us and how very proud of us she is. She said that with every smile.

May 26, 2010—I've spent the past few months slowly clearing out Mama's closets. She's kept everything, and last week I came across Daddy's wallet, some love letters between him and Mama, and the tears flooded. Mama's Parkinson's (eight years now) is worsening, but we can still make her laugh, and that smile can move mountains, wow! She's so beautiful when she flashes that "movie star" smile.

Good or bad, happy or sad, life is a journey and we must celebrate each tiny moment. Rummaging through my writings, I discovered this piece that was written in October 2010 describing one of the more difficult times with the disease.

Another Day

I'm so afraid if I don't begin to write some of this, it may fade away. Funny how two people can remember something so differently. A visit to the fair for one may bring recollection of the red wool sweater they wore and to another, how nice the Ferris wheel operator was. For fear of forgetting the important things, I'll chance writing it all!

About eight years ago, Mama was diagnosed with Parkinson's and Lewy body dementia. We knew from the start that it fluctuated, so we could expect good days and bad days. At first, good days were just as good as they had ever been. While bad days meant she'd repeat herself and shake a little in her right hand. Parkinson's will typically stay at a certain level and then drop to another, regarding a patient's functionality. For example, for about a year we could count on her trying to make sentences then we'd decipher what we thought she was trying to say. When she "dropped" to another level, all of a sudden she couldn't make sentences unless they were very short or even "yes" or "no" answers. In other words, it didn't change a little each day; it would be the same for a long time and then no more.

The worst part about that is you never knew when would be your last day to expect her to be herself. Last Thursday we had a scare. On Thursday night while taking her medicine, she choked and they were afraid she had aspirated. The ambulance came and took her to the hospital. After X-rays, they allowed her to go home, stating there was no fluid in her lungs. We were singing on a five-day trip and not able to get home. When we called on Friday morning, she wasn't responding and wasn't eating or drinking. After talking with her doctors and a home healthcare nurse, we agreed she needed to be placed back into the hospital to avoid dehydration. Again, they picked her up by ambulance and took her back to the hospital. Jeff and I were so afraid this may be another "drop" in her health level, but neither of us spoke it aloud. After advice and discussion, we as a family decided it was time for a feeding tube placement. The surgery was scheduled for Tuesday morning. We came in from our trip late Monday night and were able to see her before visiting hours ended. She looked so frail…so sick. I was prepped and ready.

She received her feeding tube on Tuesday morning, and we received instruction on how to use it. Pretty simple! Wednesday morning, she would be released as long as there was a hospital bed in place in her home.

Jeff made the calls and we went up to rearrange her furniture to accommodate the bed. It was delivered, and as the attendant began to assemble the bed, I began to see the puzzle that was being constructed. I wanted to scream "Stop," but I couldn't. I went to my bedroom in Mama's house and cried like a little girl.

After the bed was put in place, we made it up with sheets, a pillow, and blanket. Mama came home Wednesday morning, and the ambulance attendees placed her in the bed. We began the routine of feedings in the tube. On Friday night, Jeff offered to feed her the first solid food, chocolate pudding. She ate the entire cup and asked for more, so we gave her applesauce.

Over the next seven days, she used the feeding tube only once. She began to laugh, make conversation, sing, sit in the recliner, and even shuffle across the floor with Jeff's support. At times she even seems better than before the incident.

Right now I feel an overwhelming sense of relief and gratitude. She hasn't "dropped" to another level. I feel we have received that much-appreciated gift called time. Thank You Lord for another day!

Hope is the thing with feathers that perches in the soul, and
sings the tune without the words, and never stops at all.

—Emily Dickinson

In the spring of 2007, a longtime fan of The Lewis Family visited one of our concerts. As he was leaving, he offered a simple question that started a creative tidal wave for Jeff and me. He waved goodbye and asked, "When are you going to do a project with Jeff & Sheri, The Lewis Family, and The Easter Brothers?" Jeff replied that it was a good idea and we'd think about it. From the moment Jeff got back on the bus until the time we reached home, we had discussed the possibility with a record company, with both families, and had chosen all ten songs and begun arranging them. This would begin a yearlong project for us and what would be the final recording ever made of my mama.

We Are Family began as a ten-song recording featuring three best-loved songs by each group and the title cut, a brand-new song written especially for the project by our good friend Woody Wright. It was our goal to arrange every song to feature at least one member of every group, and that became the most beautiful part of the recording. It has been said by many that there is nothing like family harmony. The incredible part of this project is that Jeff and I have a family style of harmony between our vocals, while Jeff sounds incredibly like his dad and uncles and I sound like Mama and her siblings.

It was so good to hear my mama sing with Jeff and his dad, or hear me sing with my cousin Lewis and Jeff's uncle, Russell. The harmonies were so moving. Jeff and I considered this a labor of love, and we worked for months arranging, recording, fixing, and mixing.

When it was Mama's time to sing, she could sing it through each time but was unable to go back in and re-record a line that might need tweaking. So Jeff had her record it multiple times, and we pulled the words or phrases that we needed. We've recorded both ways over the years, but the latter method is more difficult for the engineer while it is easier and more emotive for the artist. Jeff worked for hours to perfect a line at a time. It was so moving to see him work so diligently at putting all this together.

By the time the project was finished, we knew we had to capture it on film. It was too special to miss. I remember one afternoon Jeff had been playing the same couple of phrases over and over and over, tweaking and editing, perfecting and arranging for literally hours. On the recording he would yell, "Y'all want to hear some more banjo?" In response, I yelled to him from the kitchen, "NOOOOOOO!" It lightened the mood to say the least.

We scheduled the video shoot during the annual Mayberry Days festival in Mt. Airy, North Carolina. On day one of the recordings, we filmed our DVD, *Mayberry Live*. On day two, all three families gathered to film b-roll for the *We Are Family* project. We sat together as a family sharing stories, funny and sad, for several hours, and later that night performed the concert of all ten songs for a live audience. The night was so special. There was much laughter and some very tender moments of tears. We were blessed to have captured what was to be Mama's final performance.

I'm a wife, a mother, a daughter, a sister, and a friend.
—Twitter/Facebook Profile, Sheri Easter

CHAPTER SIXTEEN

Halfhearted

In today's style of fast food, one-hour dry cleaning, and overnight shipping, we as writers are discovering new ways to communicate with brevity. My kids started social networking as soon as it began. After a couple of months, I became interested enough to participate, and it has become one of my favorite pastimes! So here—in short, 140 characters or less—is pretty much the way my life breezed by in 2010.

Facebook/Twitter

My status in 2010

January 8

I'll never forget the look on the faces of the folks up North who were with us in the elevator in the early '80s when my aunt asked me to mash the button...I didn't understand their confusion. I thought everyone mashed buttons. Turns out some folks press buttons!

January 11

Sheri Easter is hiding from her office work, shhh, don't tell it I'm on FB!

January 12

The house is quiet and Jeff and I are "settling down for a long winter's nap"!

January 16

Sheri Easter is blessed!

January 21

"Windshield wipers, slappin' out a tempo, keeping perfect rhythm with the song on the radio"...one of the greatest lines ever marrying lyrics with rhythm—I think about it every time it rains!

January 25

I-20, heading home

February 8

Feeling a little more like myself

February 16

Just found out our new single, "Born to Climb," is #1! So grateful for messages of encouragement

March 11

I'm starting to see a vacation in my near future and it looks so good!

March 27

I can hear Wal-Mart calling me…

April 5

First official day of spring break…after a visit to the doctor for some antibiotics and a day in the office to get this week's work done, I'll be on my way to seeing how lazy I can become. Believe it or not…not an easy task for me, chill, Sheri, chill!

April 6

Got antibiotics, office work is complete. Now at the lake house playing Scattergories with family and friends…sounds like lazy to me!

April 8

So lazy that after the past four days, I just wanna take a nap… spring break, successful!

April 9

It's so easy to smile on a sunny day!

April 10

One hour at Chuck E. Cheese = exhilaration for Maura, thereby a feeling of "win" for Jeff and me! Not too shabby for under $20!

April 11

Getting ready to watch *The Notebook*. My family says I've seen it b4. There's a strange irony in forgetting you saw a movie about Alzheimer's.

April 14

So proud of @maddyfatty musician of the year award! Thanks to all who voted.

April 17

Big hugs to The Perrys for lunch today...lots of love coming your way!

April 20

Harmony Honors were wonderful tonight! Got to hug a lot of longtime friends, I am blessed.

April 21

Dove Awards Southern Gospel Song of the Year, "Born to Climb"…praise God from whom all blessings flow!

-Gyro sandwich with cucumber sauce. I've just been transported back to 1981, University of Georgia and "cool."

-A voice inside my head tells me I'm funny…sometimes that voice is unreliable.

April 24

Heading to Myrtle Beach for an early morning concert in hopes of feeling sand on my feet before the day ends!

April 25

-Just took a midnight stroll on the beach! Deep breath, then aaahhhhhhh!

April 30

Watched my girl sing her heart out in "Copacabana" tonight at LCHS…go Morgan, you totally rocked. So proud of you! Xxxooo's

May 4

This is the first tweet from my iPad! Happy Mother's Day to me! Thanks to Jeffrey, Maura, @maddyfatty, and @morganeaster!

May 10

Awesome Mother's Day weekend! Our homecoming concert was incredible. Great crowds and artists! Raised lots of money for the homeplace!

May 11

Taping today at the Fontanel Mansion, formerly Barbara Mandrell's home...beautiful home, beautiful dinner with friends!

May 12

Just finished the newest Gaither taping. Cried so much my eyes ache. Sure sign of a great video! Proud of Morgan and her first video here!

May 14

Wow, too busy for FB is just too busy! Hello to all, love, hugs, and kisses back to each of you!

July 1

Pray for friends!

July 2

Just got back from the hospital seeing the Bowlings. They're very blessed and in good spirits. Please continue to pray for their recovery.

July 4

Celebrating Independence! Grateful for those whose sacrifice has made it possible. God bless America.

July 6

Poolside, reading, writing, swimming, sunning, eating, and a late-night fireworks show…kinda!

July 9

Beanblossom, IN, enjoying a golf cart and old friends!

July 15

Clean house means I can sit by the pool and Facebook with absolutely no guilt. S.M.I.L.E!

July 16

Traveling to Ohio, my husband says I can wake up in a mall parking lot if I want to…I want to!

July 17

Congratulations to our sweet drummer, Kyle, and his wife, Alyssa, on the birth of their baby girl, Addilyn Belle Calloway!

July 19

It's 1 a.m. here after a long day. Maura yells at us from the den. "Okay. So who's tired?" My hand is up! Night all!

July 27

My son has discovered DIY, hooray for me!

August 3

In the studio making beautiful music with my sweet husband!

August 11

Praying for sweet friends, Libbi and Tracey Stuffle! Please join me.

August 12

Keep praying for Tracey and Libbi. Tracey goes in for bypass surgery in a few moments.

August 13

Postponed Tracey's surgery until tomorrow, so keep praying saints!

August 14

Lake house…slept in, coffee in hand with absolutely nothing to do, oh yeah!

August 17

A little sad today, please keep the Tanenbaum family in your prayers. Dr. T has been our children's pediatrician for the past 22 years. Rest in peace. You are loved.

August 19

Little black snake under my house, please leave, you were not invited and I'm not happy about your visit!

September 4

Blessed!

September 5

Branson, MO, and the Silver Dollar City folks spoil us rotten. Love you guys, wow, record-breaking crowd tonight! Come see us again tomorrow ☺

September 8

Search Jeff & Sheri Easter, click "Like," and enjoy frequent music-related updates from our official Jeff & Sheri Easter Facebook page!

September 17

NQC was awesome again tonight, now night-night kisses from Maura and I'm out!

September 18

Southern Gospel 100 years celebration…oh my! Best two hours I've spent in a long time! We laughed, cried, hugged, and loved and I became a child again! Sweet memories ☺

September 23

Pushups, sit-ups, Jillian, Leslie, and an hour later I don't feel very fresh…fit, yes, fresh, not so much!

September 26

Ate at Chili's across the room from Charlene Darling and Thelma Lou…the wonderful things you see in Mayberry!

September 28

Our buddy Tony Greene is at peace. Time of death 4:25 p.m.

October 1

Louisiana bound! Think I'll sleep late in the morning…cause I can!

October 3

Forrest, MS, last night with friends and today in Montgomery, AL. Thank God for friends who are there to help you through the tough days.

October 5

Almost home, sang for our sweet friend Tony Greene's home-going tonight. Missing our buddy!

October 7

Office work followed by a massage! I should do that more often...

October 8

About to celebrate my sweet baby's birthday with a bus party! She turns five on Monday, but we have to sing all day every day between now and then. Two days at Myrtle Beach, then two days at Dollywood, so party NOW...

-I'd appreciate prayers for my sweet Mama. They took her to the hospital tonight, but she's back home now and doing okay...It's just hard being away from her when she needs me.

October 9

Maura just crawled up in my bed and prayed that "Jesus would come to the hospital and fix Grandma"; I love how she talks to God!

-Thanks so much for your prayers for Mama. She's back at the hospital, our choice, and hopefully tomorrow will be hydrated and doing better. I'm grateful for friends who pray me through, night all!

October 10

Bound for Dollywood!

October 15

Mama came home Wednesday morning. She's doing very well and adapting to a feeding tube. I can tell she's a little stronger every day.

October 16

Mama sang with us tonight, laughed (a lot), and talked about everything we talked about. Even ate Jello and applesauce and loved it! Wonderful how the smallest of things can bring joy with the right perspective!

October 17

Sang in Bradenton, FL, tonight with our sweet friend Russ Taff. Just doesn't get any better than that! I'm a fan for over thirty years now and have the 8-track to prove it! Go Russ!

October 27

WOW! Do I have the greatest friends or what? I've read every message. I've laughed. I've cried. I've remembered and it's good! Many blessings to you all! Love and hugs back at ya...

November 2

Watched my sweet Maura at ballet and tap today! Missing Jeffrey…he and Addison went to see the Colts play tonight…Go Colts!

November 3

As much as I'd like to think it is…Facebook is not getting my house cleaned, so I must walk away!

November 4

Traveling to Fredricton, NB, Canada. 1600 miles from home… coat, boots, and scarf…check!

November 5

About to cross the border and running right on time…pray for a quick and easy crossing. Sometimes it takes minutes, sometimes hours! Counting on your prayers!

November 11

Oooohhhhhh! Check out my Christmas pictures that Shannon took this morning. Love my buddies Brandon and Christa Beene for giving me a couple days of their time and tons of their creativity! Now my house is beckoning Christmas!

November 20

Kinston, NC, tonight with Guy Penrod and Taranda Greene. Just find myself missing Tony this weekend. He always made us laugh!

December 21

My sweet Mama is staying with us until Christmas Eve! Merry Christmas to us ☺

December 24

Christmas Eve…aaaahhhhhhhh!

December 28

Blessed beyond measure!

CHAPTER SEVENTEEN

With All of My Heart

In March 2008, we began a new journey that we celebrate today. Greg and Charlotte Ritchie left our group after many years of traveling with us, leaving positions open for harmony vocals and drums. At fourteen years of age, Morgan took on the full responsibility of third part vocalist for our group. We hired Kyle Calloway as our new drummer.

Today we perform with every member of our immediate family in addition to our daughter-in-law, Shannon, who is my assistant, helps at the product table, and performs occasionally; our drummer, Kyle; and our driver, Tyler Huff, longtime friend of Madison. Madison and Morgan are sharing harmony vocals with Jeff and me. Madison plays electric guitar, acoustic guitar, and mandolin onstage while Maura makes her appearance nightly singing a song, sharing a joke, and playing drums on one song with Kyle. It is as it has always been with Jeff and me—a family thing!

In December 2010, Madison married his high school sweetheart of six years, Shannon Norman, in a beautiful double-ring ceremony held at the historic Sacred Heart Cultural Center in Augusta, Georgia. Shannon is a wonderful addition to our family, and I tell folks that I began praying for her while I was carrying Madison. I heard a preacher say that the time to begin praying for this child and his mate was while he was yet in the womb. As a family, we agree God truly outdid Himself with the answer to that prayer. I am grateful for the happiness of my son and his beautiful wife.

In February 2011, we attended the Grammys for our second career Grammy nomination for our project *Expecting Good Things*. This was the project recorded during the ugliness of breast cancer, surgeries, and chemotherapy in 2008. The songs are filled with encouragement crying out from hearts that had been broken. They are filled with celebration of the end of a very difficult journey. They are filled with perspective from eyes wide open. The project is an honest musical diary from the raw and hurtful places we had journeyed.

May 16, 2011—I'm working on my book. Sometimes I wonder if it'll ever be done...by the grace of God. Madison and Shannon had a beautiful wedding ceremony in December. High school sweethearts for six years, they will be celebrating seven years together this fall. Morgan is finishing her junior year of high school this week. Get ready, senior year, wow! Maura is now enrolled in kindergarten and will be starting this fall. I giggle remembering our words of celebration thinking we'd never have to drive to the elementary school again—never say never!

As I write this final chapter, I am celebrating three years cancer-free. I am grateful for birthdays and sunshine. I am grateful to be able to exercise, which is the only thing that substantially reduces the risk of cancer. I am grateful for my family and for the songs that lift me daily.

Jeff has been the most patient and kind caregiver throughout the journey. I thought when we first married that I loved him because we had a rare and special gift. After our tenth wedding anniversary, I thought we loved each other because we shared so much in common. After the twenty-fifth anniversary, I decided I loved him because every day we wake up and make a new commitment to love. Life can be very difficult. We walk through journeys of breast cancer, deaths, and sicknesses of those we love, as well as everyday trials, and we do so holding each other up all along the way. I am grateful for a husband who loves me.

Morgan is a rising senior devoted to her drama class, and Maura is entering kindergarten this fall and learning to ride a bicycle today. My girls both have a passion for caring for others. Morgan loves the stage, and whether she sings with us, or sings, acts, and dances for her high school musicals, she does it all from her heart. Maura is probably going to be the most like her Mama. She is the eternal optimist. The other day, her sister-in-law, Shannon, complained that the battery on her cell phone was down to 12 percent. Maura responded with, "Well, twelve is still better than one!" I am grateful for the passion and optimism of my girls.

I am grateful for good memories and for words that allow us to create the intimacy in our lives. We are blessed to be able to share our hearts with those we love. By choosing "a word fitly spoken," we are able to view "apples of gold in pictures of silver" according to Proverbs 25:11. Choose your words carefully, and share your heart from its deepest places, allowing every word, every phrase, to take root in the heart of another.

To Contact Sheri:

P.O. Box 160

Lincolnton, Georgia 30817

www.jeffandsherieaster.com

Like her on Facebook, author page

Follow her on Twitter, @sherieaster

For Bookings:

Beckie Simmons Agency

5543 Edmondson Pike #10

Nashville, TN 37211-5808

(615) 595-7500

www.bsaworld.com

Jeff and Sheri support the work of Compassion International.
To sponsor a child, visit www.compassion.com

To make a tax-deductible gift to The Lewis Family Homeplace
Restoration Fund:

P.O. Box 160

Lincolnton, Georgia 30817

Publicly : Aaron Crisler · The Judy Nelon Group

615-474-8673 · aaron@nelonpr.com

I believe in Christianity as I believe that the sun has risen:

not only because I see it, but because by it

I see everything else.

—C.S. Lewis

My Prayer for You

Heavenly Father, because I have known Your goodness and Your
mercy, may these words express the fullness of my heart so that
the reader could find a deep-rooted joy and trust in You and You
alone. Life can sometimes be very difficult. I am grateful for
a family who taught me Your words and Your promises. May
I share them with those I meet each day, and may they see the
witness in the works of Your hands. I am grateful for these and
many more opportunities to allow others to *Hear My Heart*,

with thanksgiving and praise.

Sheri Easter

For God so loved the world, that he gave his only begotten

Son, that whosoever believeth in him should not perish,

but have everlasting life.

John 3:16 (KJV)

For I am not ashamed of the gospel of Christ: for it is the

power of God unto salvation to every one that believeth;

to the Jew first, and also to the Greek.

Romans 1:16 (KJV)

For whosoever shall call upon the name of the

Lord shall be saved.

Romans 10:13 (KJV)

JEFF & SHERI EASTER

J eff & Sheri Easter's latest release, *Expecting Good Things*, embraces the sentiment by which this energetic southern gospel couple lives. Their new project is a viable, precision-produced recording that musically gratifies even the most demanding enthusiast's tastes—while staying true to the bluegrass/progressive country/bluesy style that has become distinctly their own.

We wake up pretty much the same way each morning. We have our routines and like it that way! But every now and then, our routine is nudged by an inconvenience—a cancelled meeting or a flat tire. Other days it's shaken to the core with the tough stuff of life—a loss or a diagnosis. Throughout the entire process of putting together this project, we have dealt with the tough stuff, the diagnosis of breast cancer, surgeries, and chemotherapy. We've experienced in vivid definition the "in sickness and in health" part of our marriage vows. Our marriage has been strengthened, our family has drawn closer, and we have discovered a new way to breathe in and breathe out. These days we wake up each morning more thankful, more alive, and expecting good things!

After twenty-six years of music and marriage, Jeff & Sheri continue to encourage hearts while setting a standard of excellence in the field of southern gospel music. Traveling now with their children— Madison on guitar and vocals, Morgan on vocals, and Maura— Jeff & Sheri have a dynamic sound/stage presence with unbelievable family harmonies and an authentic ability to communicate a message of hope.

Whether you're listening for the first time or have been a faithful follower for years, *Expecting Good Things* is bound to touch your soul. It's hard to find in today's market anything quite as pleasant as what you'll find here. Even the album jacket beckons you for a closer look. But be prepared... you're about to be blown away. *Expecting Good Things* is just that good.

BIOGRAPHY

For Jeff & Sheri, gospel music is genetically programmed into their DNA. As members of acclaimed musical families—Jeff's father is one of the Easter Brothers and Sheri's mother is a member of The Lewis Family—they grew up surrounded by the sound of people praising God through their musical gifts.

In August of 1984, both were at the Albert E. Brumley Sundown to Sunup Gospel Singing in Arkansas. Jeff, who was playing bass for The Singing Americans at the time, took the opportunity to reintroduce himself to Sheri's mother, Polly; they had met on a previous occasion. Polly introduced Jeff to Sheri, and the two were married ten months later.

They traveled and performed as part of The Lewis Family for several years. But in 1988 they decided it was time to strike out on their own, and they haven't looked back since. Also joining Jeff & Sheri on the road is their son, Madison, who plays electric guitar for the group, and their daughter Morgan, who sings the harmonies.

Maura Grace, the newest addition to the family, is a regular highlight of Jeff & Sheri's program, and Kyle Calloway plays drums.

Jeff & Sheri have been nominated for numerous Dove Awards and won six. They've also received multiple Grammy nominations, and Sheri has been named Singing News Favorite Alto eleven times and the Singing News Female Vocalist four times. Jeff & Sheri's wall of awards also includes three Society for the Preservation of Bluegrass Music Association Awards, two International Country Gospel Music Association Awards, nine Voice Awards for Christian Country Group, four Hearts Aflame Awards, and three Cash Box awards. They have also participated in the *Gaither Homecoming* video series since 1993, which has sold over 15 million units.

Apart from their frequent appearances on the Gaither Homecoming tour and videos, Jeff & Sheri have a fairly heavy touring schedule of their own. "When we perform, we want people to leave a little different than when they came in," Sheri explains. "We want them to have a great time smiling, laughing, crying, and healing. We want them to know God loves them and that He is in control."

ACCOMPLISHMENTS

Grammy Nomination (1992) Best Southern Gospel Album, *Pickin' the Best Live*

Grammy Nomination (2011) Best Southern, Country, or Bluegrass Gospel Album, *Expecting Good Things*

21ˢᵗ Annual Dove Award (1990) Country Album of the Year—*Heirloom*

30ᵗʰ Annual Dove Award (1999) Country Album of the Year—*Work in Progress*

33ʳᵈ Annual Dove Award (2002) Country Recorded Song—"Goin' Away Party"

40ᵗʰ Annual Dove Award (2009) Bluegrass Recorded Song—"They're Holding Up the Ladder" and Bluegrass Album of the Year—*We Are Family* featuring The Lewis Family, The Easter Brothers, and Jeff & Sheri Easter

41ˢᵗ Annual Dove Award (2010) Southern Gospel Song of the Year—"Born to Climb"

Singing News Fan Awards (1991-1997, 2001, 2002, 2004, & 2008) Favorite Female Alto: Sheri Easter

Singing News Fan Awards (1995-1998) Favorite Southern Gospel Female: Sheri Easter

Singing News Fan Awards (2010) Horizon Individual: Morgan Easter

SGN Music Awards (2010) Musician of the Year: Madison Easter

Absolutely Gospel Music Awards (2011) Musician of the Year: Madison Easter

Cash Box Awards (1989) Southern Gospel Female Vocalist and Southern Gospel New Female Vocalist: Sheri Easter, and Southern Gospel Duo of the Year

The Society for the Preservation of Bluegrass Music in America (1987, 1989, 1990) Female Vocalist of the Year, Contemporary: Sheri Easter

ICGMA (1994) Ms. ICGMA Georgia and Top Female Vocalist: Sheri Easter

The Voice (1990, 1992-1998, 2000) Female Vocalist of the Year: Sheri Easter

The Voice (1996-1997) Christian Country Group

The Voice (1994) Christian Country Song: "No Limit"

The Voice (1996) Christian Country Song: "Let the Little Things Go"

The Voice (1997) Christian Country Song: "Ever Since I Gave My Heart to You"

Gospel Line Fan Pick Awards (2001) Mixed Group

SGM FanFair/USGN Fan Awards (2006) Favorite Duet

SGM FanFair/USGN Fan Awards (2005, 2006) Favorite Alto: Sheri Easter

SGN Scoops Diamond Awards (2005, 2007, 2011) and Duet (2008) Female Vocalist: Sheri Easter

SGN Scoops Diamond Awards (2003) Bluegrass Gospel Artist

SGN Scoops Diamond Awards (2010) Christian Country Group of the Year and Bluegrass Gospel Artists of the Year, (2011) Mixed Group of the Year

Southern Gospel News (2004) Special Event Project of the Year and Female Group of the Year—*Best of Friends*: Joyce Martin, Karen Peck Gooch, & Sheri Easter

Hearts Aflame Awards (1995) Album of the Year: *Thread of Hope* and Song of the Year: "Thread of Hope"

Hearts Aflame Awards Concept Video of the Year: *Let the Little Things Go*

#1 Cash Box (November 18, 1989) "You'll Reap What You Sow"

#1 CCM Update Inspirational Song (June 7, 1989) "Prayer Warrior"—*Heirloom*

#1 Southern Gospel Insight (June 10, 1991) "I Wonder If He Ever Cries"

#1 Christian Country (April-September 1993) "There Is a Way"

#1 CCM Christian Country "Singing in My Soul"

#1 Gospel Voice (Feb 2001) "We're Not Gonna Bow"

#1 Power Source Christian Country (August 1999) "Been There, Done That"

#1 Southern Notes (December 1994) "Thread of Hope"

#1 US Gospel News "Praise His Name"

#1 Singing News (February 2007) "Over and Over" & (April 2010) "Born to Climb"

In addition, over the past twenty-six years, Jeff & Sheri have produced over fifty Top 20 songs, numerous Dove Award nominations, and acquired various merits for outstanding character, humanitarian efforts, and charitable giving.

- Jeff & Sheri custom version of *The Adventure Bible*, Zondervan Bible Publishers (1991)
- Cover appearances on *Singing News, US Gospel News*, and *Homecoming* magazines
- Appearances on TNN's *Nashville Now,* Music City Tonight, The Grand Ole Opry, Trinity Broadcasting Network, Gospel Music Channel, Daystar, and Inspirational Network
- Appearance on the television series *Touched by an Angel*, "Shallow Water Part I & Part II"—Sheri in the role of Kay Winslow as part of Bill Gaither's Homecoming artists
- Regulars on Bill Gaither's *Homecoming* video series since 1993 & live tour dates since 1992

- Southern Gospel Music Guild—Jeff Easter, former board member
- Southern Gospel Music Association—Sheri Easter, board member
- PSGMA Membership—Jeff Easter
- Southern Gospel Songwriters' Association—Sheri Easter
- Hosts of INSP's series Gospel Music Southern Style (2010)
- Established The Lewis Family Homeplace Restoration Project and concert series, a non-profit organization honoring the legacy of The Lewis Family.
- Representatives for Compassion International
- 2011 HARMONY HONOR Special Recipient celebrating 25 years in Southern Gospel Music by the Southern Gospel Music Guild.

DISCOGRAPHY

1987 New Tradition

1988 Homefolks

1988 Heirloom (Sheri with Candy Hemphill Christmas and Tanya Goodman Sykes)

1989 Picture Perfect Love

1990 Brand New Love

1991 Shining Through

1992 Pickin' the Best Live

1993 The Gift

1994 Thread of Hope

1995 Silent Witness and compilation project, By Request

1996 Places in Time

1997 Sheri (solo)

1998 Work in Progress

1999 Sittin' on Cloud Nine

2000 Ordinary Day and compilation project, Through the Years

2001 It Feels Like Christmas Again

2002 My Oh My

2003 Forever and a Day

2003 Best of Friends (Sheri with Karen Peck Gooch and Joyce Martin)

2004 Sunshine

2005 Miles & Milestones

2006 Life Is Great & Gettin' Better

2008 We Are Family (Jeff & Sheri with The Easter Brothers & The Lewis Family)

2008 Mayberry Live

2010 Expecting Good Things

2010 Live at Oak Tree Studios

2011 Silver (A Twenty-Fifth Anniversary Celebration)

Also available on eBook and Audio Book

You can own the project recorded during Sheri's battle with

breast cancer, a CD filled with hope and ecouragement.

Available now at <u>www.jeffandsherieaster.com</u>